IF YOU DON'T BELIEVE ME...

LESSONS LEARNED FROM LISTENING TO THE GREATS

BY SAM ADAMS

A Books to Believe In Publication
All Rights Reserved
Copyright 2013 by Sam Adams

No part of this book may be reproduced or transmitted in any form or by any means, electronic or mechanical, including photocopy, recording or by any information storage and retrieval system, without permission, in writing from the publisher.

Proudly Published in the USA by
Books to Believe In
17011 Lincoln Ave. #408

Parker, CO 80134
Phone: (303)-794-8888
Fax: (720)-863-2013

Find Sam on both at

www.facebook.com/IfYouDontBelieveMe

Follow Sam on Twitter at
@SamAdamsComedy
#SamAdamsComedy

Find us on Facebook at
www.facebook.com/Books2BelieveIn

Follow our blog at
bookstobelievein.wordpress.com
BooksToBelieveIn.com

Follow us on Twitter at
@books2believein
#BooksToBelieveIn

ISBN: 1530319579

To
Perry & Bobbi
Peace always!!
Sam Adams

TRIBUTES

"My friendship with Sam Adams goes back more than 20 years. During that time, we've had countless conversations and shared many laughs. Through the ups-and-downs of an NFL career, I developed great trust, respect and appreciation for him. Blending an uncanny ability to mix humor with keen insight and knowledge, Sam is a one-of-a-kind storyteller.

"Whether as a reporter, columnist, TV/radio host, author or comedian, Sam's talent and wit are evident in all he does. Heck, he's even a legendary Pop-A-Shot basketball player!

"I may not be very popular in Cleveland, but I know I've got at least one friend from that city: Sam Adams."

John Elway
Executive Vice-President of Football Operations
Denver Broncos Football Club

"Of all the lessons Sam has learned from the greats, I'm certain he's never received one from a golf pro—or worse, he might have gotten tips from Charles Barkley, for whom he once caddied. No matter. Sam's enthusiasm makes him a fun golf partner and also enhances his proficiency as a writer, reporter, comedian, commentator and raconteur. To all these roles, he imparts wit, intelligence and humility; to every job, he consistently brings his "A" Game and never takes a mulligan. We could all learn a lesson or two from him."

Jon Rizzi, Editor,
Colorado AvidGolfer

"Sam Adams was one of the most insightful, creative and probing sports writers I have followed. His penchant for going deeper on a subject brought sports to life and fed my insatiable appetite for the adventure and information on my favorite teams and players."

Michael B. Hancock, Mayor
City & County of Denver

Acknowledgements

I would like to offer sincerest thanks to Jim Herre, Taylor Scott, Bob Smith, Mike Bialas, Lonnie Porter, Irv Brown, Woody Paige, Barry Forbis, Gil Spencer, Bob Burdick and John Temple—for opening doors, offering support and providing me opportunities to succeed.

I offer sincere thanks—to every coach, athlete, trainer, sports information director and school administrator I ever encountered while covering high school and college sporting events.

My sincerest thanks—to every coach, athlete, trainer, front office executive, public relations staff member and team owner I ever encountered while covering professional sports. I give sincere thanks to every reporter, broadcaster and photojournalist I encountered and befriended during my career. I offer special thanks to photographers Eric Weber, Bernard Grant, Barry Gutierrez, Paul Maynard, Linda McConnell, Wonderworks Studio, Lance Iversen/The San Fransico Chronicle, Steve Nowland, Chip Bromfield/Pro-Motion Ltd. and Kristin Rucker—each of whom have photographs that appear throughout this book. I give special thank you shout-outs to "Team Tarantino"— Andre Shaw, Kevin Huhn and Jon Rizzi—for lending their eyes and giving their time and expertise to help get me through this project.

I also offer most heartfelt and sincere thanks to all of my colleagues from *The Denver Post, Rocky Mountain News, Charlotte Observer and Colorado AvidGolfer* magazine—with a meaningful thank you to each and every person who took time out of their day to read my work in those publications.

I have many, many thanks to give Books to Believe In—I'll always remember our first time. And I would be remiss if I did not offer a most humble thank you to Valerie Adams, who supported my career pursuits through good times and bad.

Lastly, I owe a huge thank you to Glenn Gardiner—a former insurance company colleague who, in 1986, said sarcastically: *"Well, if you think you know so much, why don't you write for a newspaper?"*

Well, Glenn ... How'd I do, dude?

DEDICATION

This book is dedicated to my mother, Ellen, and the memory of my late father, Samuel Sr., as well as my entire family—most especially, my son Andrew, and my late uncle, George Rufus Adams.

That's right, Uncle George, "Butchie Bango" wrote a book.

Table of Contents

Foreword	13
Introduction	17
#1. Fame and Fortunate	24
#2. Color of Respect	37
#3. One in Particular	51
#4. To Fathers, With Glove	63
#5. Accounting For Greatness	74
#6. Ways of the World	98
#8. Basketball Jones	111
#9. Location Location	123
#10. Know When to Say Win	134
#7. Make No Mistake	146
Afterword	160
About the Author	164

Foreword

by Drew Litton

It's not easy working next to a comedian. Imagine Robin Williams or Chris Rock sitting in the desk across from yours. Actual work becomes irrelevant. Gasping for air between fits of hysterical laughter becomes part of your job description. Missed deadlines often are followed by these words to the boss: "*Sam made me do it.*" Such was my existence sitting in the cubicle next to Sam Adams during our days together on the staff of the *Rocky Mountain News*.

Before Sam embarked on his career as a comedian, he was one great sports writer. He covered Super Bowls, Final Fours, Stanley Cup Finals, World Series and Olympics. He talked to hundreds of famous people, from Tiger Woods to Paul Newman, and took pictures with many of them for "The Wall" (more on that in a minute.) And he wrote amazing stories about each of them. As a writer, Sam understood one very important fact: No matter who you are or what you do — no matter if you are a member of the Hall of Fame or the guy mopping the halls of the Hall — we all put our pants on one leg at a time. And we each have a story to tell.

Sam was smart enough to write them down, and write them down incredibly well. You're about to read a bunch of 'em. But hang with me. I've got a few of my own on this guy.

If You Don't Believe Me...

One of my favorite Sam stories involved his first real "encounter" with a Denver legend, some guy named John Elway. I won't spoil the story here because, well, Sam tells it much better than I do later in this book. Suffice to say it left me in stitches. It still does. I'm thinking, if you aren't John Elway, you'll find it pretty funny, as well.

As I mentioned earlier, everyone Sam wrote about became part of what I lovingly called "The Wall." Think of it as Sam's very own personal scrapbook, or, if you will, his version of "The Louvre." On his cubicle wall, Sam pinned pictures of everyone famous that he somehow managed to meet, interview and write about.

John Elway and Sam. Magic Johnson and Sam. Bill Cosby and Sam. George Washington and Sam. You get the idea. There was one picture of Sam with Buck O'Neil, the former Negro Leagues great. The picture really made me jealous because I'm a HUGE Buck O'Neil fan. And Sam made sure I saw the picture of him with Buck O'Neil. Every. Single. Day.

Negro Leagues great John "Buck" O'Neil

Sam Adams

Something you should know about Sam: he is an incredibly generous soul. He's always doing something for a good cause, always willing to give of himself. Sam is the kind of guy who would "almost" give you the shirt off his back. Notice I said "almost." Sam has this fantastic letterman's jacket, one he was given during O'Neil's visit to Denver for a Negro Leagues Museum fundraiser. I coveted the jacket, lusted after it and begged for it something awful. Sam wouldn't give up the jacket. But I digress.

What makes this book so great is, besides the fact it's full of amazing and often hilarious stories, it's also about a sports writer in the midst of Denver's sports history. The John Elway Era. The Patrick Roy Era. The Broncos winning Super Bowls Era. And The World is Coming to an End Era. (That would be 2007 — the year the Colorado Rockies went to the World Series). Sam was like Forrest Gump, popping up throughout the big moments during the golden age of Colorado sports. And he has the pictures to prove it.

The pictures. There was one of Sam and Denver Broncos great Floyd Little. The day after the picture went up on "The Wall," I received a signed copy of Little's new biography in the mail. Boy, was I in heaven. Sam had his picture. I had an *autographed* copy of Little's book to brag about — a book that consisted of a nice, personal 14-word inscription and autograph from a future Pro Football Hall of Famer. Oh, how I let Sam know it!

A few weeks later, Sam came waltzing into the office with his very own signed copy of Little's book. Fine. "But mine has more words than yours," I said beaming, with pride. Sam handed me his copy of the book. I opened it to read: *"To Sam, Thanks for your kindness and friendship. Floyd Little #44 ... Plus 15 words."* Sam had out-done me again.

There's one more story about Sam to share. It became known as the "Great Cookie Dough Caper" in the *Rocky Mountain* News' newsroom. Sam, because he is such a

15

great guy, purchased some oatmeal raisin cookie dough to help a co-worker's relative in her school's fundraising efforts.

Sam asked the seller to store the cookie dough in the office's break-room refrigerator—which he thought would be a safe place. If you have ever stored anything in your office's refrigerator, you know this was a bad idea. If your food is not contaminated with hazardous bacteria from uncleaned surfaces, then it is sure to get swiped by someone who didn't bring a meal to work.

Sam's oatmeal raisin cookie dough went missing. He was NOT a happy camper about it. Who could blame him? It's pretty weak, stealing someone's cookie dough out of the office fridge. Sam even made a video appeal, comical albeit, that aired on the newspaper's Web site. The perpetrator was never apprehended. But I have a theory, one I feel you might agree with after reading this book.

John Elway did it.

Introduction

*"Have confidence.
You can't be Sam without it ... "*
~Bill Cosby

On October 7, 2007 I sat in Bill Cosby's dressing room at the Pikes Peak Center in Colorado Springs. For me, at that time, a 21-year veteran sports writer with six years of experience in stand-up comedy, it was a mildly extraordinary setting.

Me, alone with the great Bill Cosby. Mr. "Noah's Ark-Chicken Heart-Fat Albert-Give me a bowl of delicious Jell-O Pudding" himself. A few days earlier, I interviewed Mr.

Cosby by telephone for my sports column in the *Rocky Mountain News*. Toward the end of our conversation, I told him that I performed stand-up comedy. He immediately extended an invitation to meet after the first of his two shows — and told me to bring a pen and note pad so that he could give me a lesson.

There was a ticket waiting for me at will call, along with directions to the security desk. After the show I was escorted to Mr. Cosby's dressing room. We shook hands, and right away he made fun of me because the Denver Broncos were getting beat by the San Diego Chargers, 41-3. I was supposed to be at the stadium covering the game. I chose to hang out with Cliff Huxtable instead.

I felt like a toddler whose feet dangled aimlessly out of a high chair while I listened to Mr. Cosby speak. It was the most meaningful 90 minutes of my comedy career — during which time I did absolutely nothing whatsoever to make an impression on this man. I just sat there — shy, speechless, thoughtless and in awe.

The lesson Mr. Cosby offered included a series of simple guidelines to follow: *"Your job is to make them laugh, and if you don't make them laugh you get an F! ... It's just a tripod — thinking, writing, performing ... Always pick things you feel funny about ... Have confidence. You can't be Sam without it ...*

"It's wide open if you want to think."

It was awesome to receive advice from the greatest comedian of all-time. He reminded me that I had not put enough thought into how far I could go in comedy — and in life — if I took the time to ... think.

◆ ◆ ◆

I gave thought to writing this book after a night of wine drinking and storytelling with friends and acquaintances. I spent the latter portion of the evening entertaining the group with details of my past interviews and celebrity encounters. The ending for each tale offered the same punchline—"And then I went home." Someone in the group suggested I write a book and call it, " ... *And Then I Went Home*."

    I laughed, and then I went home—with thoughts about writing a book in my head. The next morning, the book-writing idea still felt fresh. I went to the closet in my "Me Room" and pulled out a bin with some old note pads, a bag full of microcassettes and two bags full of press passes. Then I took a few glances into scrapbooks filled with articles I had written about high school games.

    My thoughts drifted back to that day in September, 1986, when I walked into *The Denver Post* building at 650 15th Street. I was on lunch break from my job as a clerk at an insurance company—Security Life of Denver. For me, the visit was all about satisfying curiosity—and saving some lunch money. I walked into the Post building well-aware that I wasn't qualified to be a staff writer.

    In fact, the only time I had ever been paid to write for anyone was during my time served in the U.S. Army, when I wrote love notes for one of the soldiers in my platoon who was too illiterate to write for himself. (It was a Cyrano de Bergerac kind of thing—except I was more like "Cyra-bro" with a much smaller nose.)

    The guard at the Post's security desk made a phone call to the sports department. Jim Herre answered. Herre was the Post's deputy sports editor. He invited me into his office, and we spoke briefly before I handed him a piece of paper with some of my writings.

◆ ◆ ◆

    While Herre read, I sat in a chair—slightly nervous and humorously distracted by the framed photograph on his wall of a high school football player in full uniform taking

If You Don't Believe Me...

a pee. Herre finished reading, turned his chair to face me and said, "We just don't hire people off the street." I wasn't disappointed because I had no expectations. He handed me his business card and advised me to call Taylor Scott, the Post's high school sports editor.

I called Scott, and he brought me on board immediately for part-time work. The first two months I spent a lot of time on the phone, calling school coaches and administrators to get statistics needed to compile box scores. The job was boring, and I was on the verge of quitting. Scott pulled me aside one night, and said he was sending me with one of the experienced prep writers to cover a basketball game the following day. I understood that it would be an audition for me, and that the veteran reporter's story was going to print.

Highland High School against Jefferson High, in a boys' basketball game played at McNichols Sports Arena on December 20, 1986. Jarad Rivera scored 10 of his game-high 20 points in the fourth quarter to lead Highland High to a 61-57 victory. I got back to the office and wrote my "audition" game story. A brief spat with Scott over a missing word in a quote made me angry enough to want to punch him in the nose. I couldn't figure out why he made such a big deal about an "audition" story until the following morning, when I saw my story in the Post.

My first byline. I was hooked.

♦   ♦   ♦

The more assignments I received from the Post, the more anxious I became about making a living as a sports writer. In the summer of 1990, the Post's executive sports editor, Woody Paige, said to me, "I like what you're doing kid, but don't quit your day job." I was 30 years old on Dec. 28, 1990 when I collected my last paycheck from my full-time employer, Great-West Life. I had quit my day job.

It was a huge gamble—especially for a husband and father with family responsibilities. But I took Paige's words as a challenge, believing that if I had more free time during the day, I could find more stories to freelance to the Post. I believed that if I wrote more stories, the Post would admire my hustle and find me worthy of being a full-time reporter on its staff.

The financial waters got rough on more than one occasion, but I never let my family's fiscal affairs reach an impecunious state. I found just enough work weekly to help keep things afloat. In February, 1992 Paige summoned me into his office. The Post's editor, Gil Spencer, also was present when Paige offered to hire me full-time. I gladly accepted the job—knowing neither Paige or Spencer had a clue that I'd quit my day job 14 months earlier.

> *"Define the goal.*
> *Decide what's important."*
> ~Woody Paige

For years, I've kept two well-tattered items in my wallet. One is a piece of paper with advice from Paige: *"Define the goal. Decide what's important."* The other is the business card Herre handed to me in 1986.

Herre moved on to work for *Sports Illustrated*. I had never asked him why he took the time to speak to me that day in '86. So I did—during a conversation that followed my surprise phone call to his office in January, 2013. My guess is, we had spoken twice in 27 years that passed since I met him in 1986. "I remember when I was in your position, walking into an editor's office," Herre said. "The same thing happened to me. Somebody gave me a break."

If You Don't Believe Me...

♦ ♦ ♦

In 23 years, I wrote about quarterbacks, linebackers and punters, gymnasts and figure skaters, skiers and swimmers, pitchers and batters, boxers and wrestlers, coaches and managers, owners and general managers, goaltenders and goalkeepers, shooting guards and shot-blockers, golfers and bowlers, equestrians and race car drivers, sprinters, hurdlers and marathoners, mushers and curlers. I reported game-winning overtime goals, buzzer-beating baskets, shutouts, last-second winning drives and stunning knockout punches ...

I covered Super Bowls held in Atlanta, New Orleans, San Diego and Miami, and Olympiads hosted in Sydney, Australia and Salt Lake City, Utah. I reported on football games played at historic Lambeau Field in the frigid cold of a Wisconsin winter, World Series games played at fabled Fenway Park in the fall and sat court-side within the walls of basketball greatness while working at UCLA's Pauley Pavilion ...

I felt 80,227 baseball fans shake the press box at Mile High Stadium after Eric Young homered in the Colorado Rockies' first-ever home at-bat. I stood on the sideline in Grover, Colorado — population 150 — to report on a 6-man football state championship game. I had a rare hangover and missed a no-hitter pitched by Jim Abbott at old Yankee Stadium. But I made it on time to cover show jumping, karate, soccer and lacrosse — and once wrote a review on a Def Leppard concert.

I saw lots of games, lots of players, heard lots of cheers after victories and listened to plenty of gripes and groans after losses. Not bad for a guy who barely graduated high school in 1977, dropped out of college in 1979, was deemed medically unfit after 34 days of service in the U.S. Army in 1980 and had no clue what lay ahead in life after Greyhound managed to lose his suitcase during the long bus ride from Cleveland to Denver in 1984.

I was quite fortunate to have people like Herre and Paige give me opportunities to develop and nurture a passion, and to meet people like Cosby who offered simple and effective words of advice. I never thought I would share pieces of my life through the pages of a book. I think you'll be pleased with the results.

As my friend, Jim Koch — the brewer of Sam Adams Beer — likes to say ... Cheers!

Cheers!

FAME AND FORTUNATE

*"If you're not enjoying life,
then what are you doing?"*
-Tim Tebow

One story I have never shared publicly—until now—is about a celebrity encounter I experienced in 1972, at Higbee's department store in downtown Cleveland.

Curiosity lured me into a long line of women who were waiting to meet Academy Award-winning actress Helen Hayes and author/screenwriter Anita Loos. They were signing copies of their new book, *"Twice Over Lightly: New York Then and Now."* I didn't want the book, nor could I afford to buy a copy of the book. I was 12 years old. I just wanted to catch a glimpse of someone famous.

It took a long while before I reached the table where Hayes and Loos were seated. At first glance, they reminded me of the Baldwin Sisters—who I'd seen on *The Waltons* television show. Both ladies autographed a small piece of paper, which Hayes handed to me.

It was quite the sight—people waiting in line to meet someone *famous*. Hayes and Loos had achieved a level of success that warranted adulation. Back then, I thought it was cool. Years later, I reached a level of success as a journalist. Granted, people didn't stand in line to meet me. But they recognized my face from the newspaper column, saw me on television and listened to me on the radio. Some asked for hand-shakes. Others asked to take pictures together. I was a former insurance clerk-turned-celebrity.

A "local" celebrity, mind you, but a celebrity nonetheless.

I must say, the perks weren't bad. The "beautiful people" around town enhanced my local celebrity status by inviting me to fundraisers, restaurant openings, fashion shows and other events of the like. I enjoyed the attention, but made sure to stay humble, knowing the wee bit of celebrity status I owned around town could vanish in Denver's thin air much sooner than later.

"You want people to like you for you—not just because you can put that ball in the hole, or you can run that football or hit that baseball. You want people to like you for being you."
~Chauncey Billups

Celebrity attention is cool, but sometimes you want to visit a restaurant, sports bar or shopping mall and not be bothered with questions that pertain to your job. You want to relax. It happened to me a few times. I could only imagine what it was like for someone who actually was famous.

National Basketball Association star Chauncey Billups once told me how hard some athletes find it to be themselves when the eyes of the public are watching.

If You Don't Believe Me...

"It's like you're a fish in a fish bowl," Billups said. "People may appreciate what you do on the court, but they don't know what you have to go through sometimes off the court. It's tough. You have to watch what you do and say in certain environments. For a guy that (acts) a certain way, it's hard to turn that switch on and off. Sometimes you just want to be you.

"You want people to like you for you — not just because you can put that ball in the hole, or you can run that football or hit that baseball. You want people to like you for being you. What happens is, what draws them to you is what you do professionally, what you do for work."

In my time spent working as a sports reporter, I witnessed a number of athletes who managed to handle their celebrity status with surprising ease. Quarterback Tim Tebow is included in that group.

In July, 2011, when Tebow was a member of the Denver Broncos, I walked alongside him for more than three hours, asking questions for *Colorado AvidGolfer* magazine while he played in a celebrity golf tournament at Lake Tahoe. One spectator called it a "mob scene, bro." Fans engulfed Tebow as he walked from tee to tee, at times tripping over themselves seeking photographs and autographs.

I thought, *really*? People flocked in droves to catch glimpses of a quarterback who barely completed 50 percent of his passes in the NFL? And his golf game ... That day, Tebow hit the golf ball the same way I had seen him throw a football for the Broncos — hard, while often missing his intended target.

Golf swings aside, Tebow was almost too good to be true. He knew when to smile, said all the right things and handled the masses with extreme politeness. "If you're not enjoying life, then what are you doing?" Tebow told me. "It doesn't matter how successful you are in whatever it is that you do, if you're not enjoying life you should change."

My life changed suddenly after the *Rocky Mountain News* closed in 2009. We knew the newspaper was on the verge of closing. We just didn't know exactly when it would happen. The owners of the paper showed up unannounced on February 26 and told us that the following day was the last for the News. Write a column. Go home. Come back tomorrow. Clean out your desk. Turn in your work badge and garage access card. Say goodbye to your colleagues. Leave the building for good.

I was 49 years old with no full-time employer. Just like that, I was back to being a "regular" dude again.

"Sometimes a man has to get his pride and integrity back by doing something constructive and positive."

~Clarence Kay

Whenever I had moments of self-pity about the paper's closing, I thought back to some of the stories I had written over the years about athletes having to start over. One, which was written in 2000, stood out among all others. It was about a former NFL player who worked at a local Grease Monkey.

Clarence Kay played tight end for the Broncos in the mid-1980s. He was a much better blocker than pass-catcher. In fact, Kay was such a great blocker that his head coach, Dan Reeves, went beyond great lengths to keep him out of jail and on the playing field.

If You Don't Believe Me...

Kay found trouble way too often. He drank alcohol. He snorted cocaine. Calls to the police to apprehend Kay came frequently. He had as many, if not more arrests on his police record (most of them related to domestic violence) than he did career touchdowns scored (13) in the NFL.

Reeves once visited Kay's home, to inform the player that he'd flunked a drug test. Kay called it the "Knock from hell."

"(Reeves) said the team would test me five times a week, and if I tested positive again I was gone," Kay told me during a series of three interviews for the News. "I told him I had no problem with it. And I had my package of cocaine under the couch he was sitting on. When he left, guess what I did? Back to the same old thing."

Kay appeared in three Super Bowls during his playing career with Denver. He wore a Denver County prison uniform when the Broncos won Super Bowl XXXII. I spent more time with Kay than any person I've ever interviewed — almost seven hours in different locations. He was contrite and humbled by his self-inflicted predicament.

Think about it. Kay had gone from having a job playing four quarters of football against teams like the Houston Oilers to working a job that required him to add four quarts of oil to a Chevy Astro van.

"People will say, 'What am I doing at Grease Monkey?'" Kay said. "Well, people who would judge me on that are going to judge the next man for killing or robbing someone. So what would you want for a young man to be?

"Maybe I'm not as functional as someone else doing what they do. Sometimes a man has to get his pride and integrity back by doing something constructive and positive."

♦ ♦ ♦

Kay's words resonated with me. Don't dwell on the past. Do something constructive and positive. For me, performing comedy full-time would be a constructive, positive—and risky—life change after the News' closing. I was content to let go of the rigors from my past "life" as a reporter. The hard part was letting go of so many memories from the job—from watching the games played to talking with the people who played them.

There was one other perk of the job as a reporter that I had to let go of—meeting celebrities from the world of entertainment. I had met many of them in various settings over the years. To this day, I am a notorious name-dropper when around friends.

◆ ◆ ◆

I talked with the great Quincy Jones. I interviewed singer Chaka Khan. Grammy-winning singer Al Jarreau once told me that I gave him the best stage introduction he had ever received. I met actor James Caan while waiting in line at a soul food restaurant in Los Angeles. I played a few mock hands of poker with actor Ben Affleck at a fundraiser for the Paralyzed Veterans of America held during the 2008 Democratic National Convention.

I solicited NFL game predictions from actress/singer Dolly Parton at a book signing, and asked comedian Sinbad to give me NFL predictions while he cooled off in his dressing room after a performance. Rapper Master P gave me his cell phone number and told me he wanted to hook up with the Broncos' running backs at Super Bowl XXXII. In a conversation with actor Dennis Quaid, he told me he'd "smoke" fellow actor Kevin Costner in a 100-meter dash.

I talked basketball with film director/New York Knicks fan Spike Lee and actress Vivica A. Fox. I talked football with actor Blair Underwood and actress/rapper

Queen Latifah. I talked baseball with Tim Russert (the late host of NBC's *Meet The Press*) at Major League Baseball's All-Star Game in 1998, and read a book to students with actress Gabrielle Union, rapper Reverend Run (of Run DMC fame) and game host Roger Lodge during the 2005 NBA All-Star Weekend.

Grammy Award-winning guitarist George Benson approached me, shook hands and started a conversation at a nightclub in Scottsdale, Arizona. I recognized Benson, but I'm sure he had no clue who I was.

I've got plenty more celebrity encounters to tell, each with a story within the story. Most of them end the same— "... and then I went home." Here are a few that I like to share in detail.

◆ ◆ ◆

As I like to tell my comedy audiences, life is all about situations and solutions. In July, 2007 I had an unexpected encounter with Costner. The Academy Award-winning actor was playing in a sponsors' round for a celebrity golf tournament at Lake Tahoe. I was on site looking to interview another actor, Don Cheadle, for *Colorado AvidGolfer* magazine.

I watched Cheadle hit balls at the driving range. The man hitting balls in a stall to his left happened to be Philip Bailey, lead singer of my all-time favorite band—Earth, Wind and Fire. I introduced myself to Bailey, who, like Cheadle, attended Denver East High School—in different years, albeit.

Bailey said he didn't know Cheadle, and he found their Denver high school connection to be a fascinating coincidence. Cheadle, on the other hand, shrugged it off as no big deal and offered exactly five minutes of his time for asking questions—hardly enough time for answers to craft a blurb, let alone a cover story.

The situation would have been bleak—except I already had a solution in hand. The day before I approached Cheadle with an interview request, Costner gave me time for an interview during the latter part of his round of golf. Costner talked about his golf game while ladies in the gallery screamed and whistled for him to sign autographs and take pictures. The closer we got to the 18th green, the more the conversation shifted toward music. Costner talked about drawing excitement from playing guitar and singing with his new band, Modern West.

"Sam, this is Paul Newman. You must get this all the time, but you're a great beer—are you an amber or just a lager?"
~Paul Newman

"As soon as that starts happening, no one can get in your way," he said. "No one. And that's a really great feeling. It's not going to get interrupted with an autograph or a handshake—not that any of those things are bad. Two hours on stage is a good moment. I don't seek to try to explain almost anything I do. I just kind of go do it. I take it seriously, so if (audiences) stumble on it, it'll be as good as I can play at that moment."

Hanging around Costner on the golf course was cool. Did I mention the time Academy Award winner Paul Newman called my home?

August 7, 2004 to be exact. Newman called me from Canada, to do an interview for the News. It was a few days before Denver hosted a Grand Prix auto race. Newman's racing team would be in town to compete. I was star-struck with laughter from his opening line.

If You Don't Believe Me...

"*Sam, this is Paul Newman. You must get this all the time, but you're a great beer — are you an amber or just a lager?*"

I answered "amber." In hindsight, "bock" would have been more accurate. It was quite the start to a very memorable conversation with a great man, an outstanding actor — and fellow native Clevelander.

At the time of our conversation Newman was 79 years old. He didn't sound like a man who looked forward to slowing down any time soon. "Well, it's nice to have two passions — three passions including my lady," Newman told me. "Although, she's not excited about (racing) as (the movies), I might add.

"I started racing very late, when I was 47. I thought owning a team would be a nice sequel. But I seem to be here with both of them now and enjoying both still. As long as I don't embarrass myself, I guess I'll stay in the driver's seat for a while."

Newman was married 50 years to actress Joanne Woodward when he died in 2008.

♦ ♦ ♦

In hindsight, I might have been better suited to report for *Entertainment Tonight*, as I seemed to be magnetized to celebrities in entertainment. But the sports world is where I thrived. Thing is, I never scored the big one-on-one interviews with icons the likes of Michael Jordan or Muhammad Ali. I had an unusual knack for getting the most cantankerous, boorish athletes to speak to me.

I've learned that perseverance can lead to prosperity — whether you're a reporter seeking an interview, or you're a fan seeking a celebrity's autograph. It's a lesson learned from my attempt to draw the attention of former Major League Baseball star Eddie Murray.

At the time (1994), Murray played for the Cleveland Indians. It was common knowledge that he did not care to speak to reporters. I managed to talk an editor at *The Denver Post* into believing I could get Murray to speak to me for our cover story about the art of switch-hitting. I believed I would interview Murray, but my real motivation for taking a trip to Cleveland on the paper's dime was to visit my mother.

I arrived at Cleveland's Hopkins Airport, drove a rental car to Municipal Stadium and made a formal interview request with the Indians' media relations department. The request was politely declined. They said I'd have to get Murray on my own. I went onto the playing field just as Murray walked toward the Indians' clubhouse after taking batting practice. I never was so hesitant to approach another human being.

"*Excuse me, Eddie ...* " Murray kept walking. I called out louder, "*Excuse me, Eddie!! ...* " He turned around, holding a baseball bat and wearing the look of a snorting bull. "Who are you—and what do *you* want?" he asked. I immediately offered my name and employer. I might have shouted my birthdate and social security number too.

> *" ... I refuse to let somebody else dictate to me or control some of my happiness."*
>
> ~Eddie Murray

I told Murray about my assignment, and that the story wouldn't be complete without talking to him. Aside from Mickey Mantle, Murray might be the greatest switch-hitter in MLB history. He finished his 21-year career with 3,255 hits—504 of them home runs.

If You Don't Believe Me...

Murray paused, then agreed to an interview. "Come by my locker in 15 minutes," he said.

It was a long 15-minute wait in the Indians' clubhouse. I went to Murray's locker, and he encouraged me to ask questions. When I did, he returned "yes" and "no" answers to each one, while poking his face into a newspaper.

Murray's teammate, journeyman infielder Rene Gonzales, snickered nearby—as if he knew I was being duped. Suddenly something changed. Unprovoked, Murray began a muttering rant about the news of the day—O.J. Simpson and the murders of Nicole Brown and Ron Goldman.

Rather than turning off my recorder and risking a clicking sound that may have brought Murray out of a self-induced trance, I covered the microphone and listened to him for nearly five minutes. He finished the rant on Simpson, put away the paper, turned to me and said, "Now what were you asking?"

I went back to the first question about switch-hitting. Murrary willingly explained how and when he started to bat from both sides. By the time we reached the end of the interview, the subject had changed to his unwillingness to speak to the media.

"Some of these guys, I see them hurt by what's written in the paper," Murray told me. "I tell them, 'Hey, you've come a long way to let those words tear you down.' Sometimes (the press) wants you to get into a battle with them. I won't do it, and that's what gets them upset."

Feeling lucky, I decided to ask Murray about his Hall of Fame chances. He laughed. "I don't control that, and I refuse to let somebody else dictate to me or control some of my happiness," he said. I left Murray's locker with not one but two stories. Now, when I drop his name, it's preceded with "Hall of Famer," as Murray was enshrined at the baseball museum at Cooperstown, New York in 2003.

> *"Enjoy life, my brotha, because it's too short."*
> ~Charles Barkley

Sometimes, the interviews are hard to get. But I found, for every surly Eddie Murray there are at least a half-dozen happy-go-lucky types like Charles Barkley.

Five months after being shoved into the unemployment line in 2009, I was offered an opportunity to caddy for the basketball Hall of Famer at the Tahoe celebrity tournament. It was a great opportunity, and I accepted. I also risked heat stroke from dragging Barkley's bag for nine holes under a hot afternoon sun.

Barkley really is an incredible dude. He played basketball with incredible athletic abilities and instincts. He just happens to wield an incredibly awful golf swing that leads to incredibly awful rounds of golf. Caddying for him was an enjoyable experience to write about because "Sir Charles" never takes himself—or others—seriously. He exchanged playful texts with Lance Armstrong before the round, cracked jokes about Michael Jordan, Tiger Woods and Oprah Winfrey during the round and playfully (I think) threatened to kick my ass toward the end of the round.

The show belonged to the "Round Mound of Rebound"—until Jordan appeared from nowhere at the 15th tee box and gave his long-time friend a verbal beat-down. It was a moment that drew laughter from everyone standing nearby. But it wasn't the highlight of the round for me. That moment occurred while Barkley and I strolled alone up the 13th fairway, when he spoke solemnly about the death of his brother earlier in the year. Darryl Barkley received a heart transplant in 2003, and died of a heart attack six years later at age 42.

"Enjoy life, my brotha, because it's too short," Barkley told me.

It was the best tip a golfer could give to his caddy.

COLOR OF RESPECT

"Sometimes it's unfortunate that the ones who pour the gasoline on the fire are the ones who get the most attention."

~Gene Washington

My original game plan for this book did not include writing a chapter about race. However, the topic became a source of inspiration after the University of Colorado fired head coach Jon Embree at the end of the 2012 season. After his firing, Embree, who was two years into a five-year contract, pointed out to the media that black men rarely receive second chances to coach Division I-A college football programs.

Every news outlet—local and national—focused on the sensitive component of race in Embree's firing. The NCAA's hiring ledger supported his claim. Forty-one black men have been hired on a full-time basis to coach Division I-A college football programs. Only one—Tyrone Willingham—has been fired and subsequently hired to coach at the Division I-A level.

More often than not, black men hired as head coaches at Division I-A schools inherit college football's version of the "fixer-upper" home—programs badly in need of repairs. The odds of instantaneous success are very low. It's a situation each coach is aware of when he accepts a job.

Embree was in that very situation. There might have been progress shown from his youthful team during practices, but the results on game day were invisible in the win-loss column. Embree's teams went 4-21 in two seasons, including 1-11 with no home wins in 2012. Eight of those 11 losses came by an average margin of 39 points.

Embree had the right temperament for taking on a "fixer-upper" program. To me, he was in over his head—a first-time head coach trying to compete with talent way too young and way too inferior to the majority of teams in the Pac-12.

Colorado's football program hasn't finished with an above-.500 record since 2005. My guess is, impatience among administrators and boosters, more than skin color, was the primary reason behind Embree's firing.

When people ask me why black men don't receive second chances to coach college football, my counter is, why are we still so low on the waiting list for first chances? Increase the number of first-chance hirings—for all minorities—and don't limit those opportunities to "fixer-upper" programs. If those new hires can buck the odds and find immediate success the first time around, it should increase patience among boosters and administrators — and cut down a need for second chances.

♦ ♦ ♦

One of my best comedy bits offers an unusual reference relative to skin color. Instead of settling for being called black or white, I suggest you go to a hardware or paint store, and match your skin with a paint swatch to find your "true" color.

I'm a shade of brown called "Sumptuous Spice." That's the comical viewpoint. The reality is, race is a very volatile topic — a topic that, over time, has left people chasing their tails for solutions. It can produce conversation that fosters an uncomfortable rigidity in some, and venomous anger from others.

> *"(Bleep) your A-List. I don't like you either. Maybe you'll get in a car wreck. Nobody is going to miss another black-ass boy ... So shove that A-List up your black stinking (bleep) ... P.S. - Your (sic) one of those half-assed educated blacks. Go back to Mississippi boy!!"*
> — Rocky Mountain News reader

If You Don't Believe Me...

In a society which chooses to address people by color, the topic seems unavoidable. Even the government needs to track us by colors—see the Census Report.

Categorizing people by color can lead to racism, which, to me, is like cancer in that we've spent years on research but haven't been able to find a cure. Racism is a proverbial flame. No one and nothing—not even sports—is exempt from its sensational burn. It can scorch you when you least expect it.

◆ ◆ ◆

I received hundreds of letters from readers during my time spent as a columnist at the *Rocky Mountain News*. I came to expect that those readers wanted to either express opinions or offer grammatical and factual corrections. I welcomed all letters, emails and telephone calls because I never was too thin-skinned to accept critique and criticism.

One day in 2005, I opened an envelope postmarked in Denver. There was no return street address. Just a first initial and last name—"J. Stolle." The legible handwritten letter contained a lot of vile comments aimed at the local professional sports teams—as well as me.

For some reason, I decided to keep the letter—maybe as a subtle reminder that there are some really ignorant people in this world. Two weeks later, I received a letter from someone named "Larry Tills." Again, postmarked in Denver with no street address. When I opened the letter I recognized the same handwriting as "J. Stolle." Again, it was a letter that offered extremely vulgar content—and a racist rant pointed directly at me.

"*(Bleep) your A-List. I don't like you either. Maybe you'll get in a car wreck. Nobody is going to miss another black-ass boy ... So shove that A-List up your black stinking (bleep) ... P.S. - Your (sic) one of those half-assed educated blacks. Go back to Mississippi boy!!*"

The insults stung, but not enough to damage my psyche. I still have six of the letters which came over three years—each in the same handwriting, no return address and different names: "J. Tritt", "Jay Pristine" and "Rueben Garcia." Most of the correspondence had it in for me, as well as the Denver Broncos.

In hindsight, I should have taken the letters to an editor at the newspaper—or called law enforcement. But I never felt like lives were being threatened, so it seemed like a waste of time. I let the idiot slide and never learned his or her true identity.

◆ ◆ ◆

Ironically, another one of the writer's main targets was Broncos' linebacker Bill Romanowski—who garnered a reputation for irritating people throughout his career. On the night of Dec. 15, 1997 Romanowski took his reputation to new heights—or lows depending on the point of view.

That night, the Broncos played the San Francisco 49ers at 3Com Park on *Monday Night Football*. Denver was 11-3 and had established itself as a solid contender to win the American Football Conference championship. The 49ers came into the game with a 12-2 record, and were strong contenders for the National Football Conference championship.

During the third quarter, Romanowski had an encounter with 49ers wide receiver J.J. Stokes. Stokes felt someone grab his crotch at the end of a play. He believed that someone was Romanowski. The two players came helmet-to-helmet when "Romo" spit at Stokes' face—a despicable act that was caught clearly by the television cameras. Stokes did not retaliate.

The 49ers went on to win the game 34-17. However, Romanowski's act would not go unnoticed—not by the Broncos, the 49ers, the National Football League, viewers of the game or the media. Stokes is black. Romanowski is white. A controversy simmered to a boil, with very little gray area in between.

There already was one race card on the table in sports when the Romanowski-Stokes incident took place. Two weeks earlier, a black player for the Golden State Warriors, Latrell Sprewell, choked his white coach, P.J. Carlesimo, during a practice.

> *"In some ways it may be a blessing in disguise—if the issue of race in sports can be dealt with in a way where people can say, 'Look, we obviously have a problem here. What can we do to use sports in a leadership position?'"*
>
> ~Gene Washington

Initially, Sprewell was suspended without pay for 10 games. Later, the Warriors decided to void his contract—which had three years and over $20 million remaining—and the National Basketball Association suspended him for one year. After arbitration, Sprewell's contract was reinstated, and his NBA-induced suspension was reduced from one calendar year to the remaining 68 games of the 1997-98 season—costing him more than $6 million in salary forfeiture.

The NFL fined Romanowski $7,500, which generated ill feelings within the Broncos' locker room from some of his black teammates who believed that a black player spitting on a white player would have resulted in a much harsher penalty. Those players' opinions may have been a direct reaction to what some perceived to be an overreaction on the part of the NBA to suspend Sprewell for 68 games without pay.

Gene Washington, from the NFL's executive offices, was responsible for levying disciplinary action against Romanowski. Washington, who is black, played wide receiver for 10 seasons in the NFL—nine with the 49ers. I spoke with him by telephone a few days after he issued Romanowski's fine.

"If J.J. had spit on Romanowski it would have been the same fine. It had nothing to do with the color. It was a despicable act," Washington told me. "This is a lightning rod for the racial tension that exists—an opportunity for people to talk about the racial tension in sports and in society. In some ways it may be a blessing in disguise—if the issue of race in sports can be dealt with in a way where people can say, 'Look, we obviously have a problem here. What can we do to use sports in a leadership position?'"

Washington was quite candid about his concerns over the element of race being added to an already-volatile spitting incident. "If people who can separate the wheat from the chaff, and really say things that are not filled with emotion or seeking reaction ... Sometimes it's unfortunate that the ones who pour the gasoline on the fire are the ones who get the most attention." he said.

◆ ◆ ◆

Race was not a factor, for me, when I began to pursue a career as a sports writer. When I was hired full-time by *The Denver Post* in 1992 I never thought, 'Wow, I'm a *black* sports writer!' I was just happy to have proven myself worthy of a full-time job.

In October, 1992 the Post sent me to San Diego to cover a Broncos-Chargers game. The Broncos lost by a field goal, 24-21. Afterward, I went into the Chargers' locker room and approached a player named Ronnie Harmon. He made one of the game's biggest plays, converting a third-and-11 pass into a 12-yard gain in the final three minutes of the fourth quarter.

Harmon's back faced me when I asked if we could talk about his contribution to the win. He turned around, looked at me, extended a hand and asked who I worked for. Still shaking my hand—and wearing a look on his face that bore some amazement—Harmon smiled and said, "It's good to see more brothers in the media."

I've never forgotten Harmon's facial expression—or his strong, prolonged handshake. Until he uttered those words, I hadn't paid much attention to the lack of blacks in the sports media—or in all media, for that matter. I should have been more aware of my surroundings. Clearly, it meant something to Harmon—and probably to other black athletes—to see the face of a black person representing the media. As time passed, I found that some black players felt more comfortable opening up to black media members.

◆ ◆ ◆

You rarely hear references to a "*white quarterback*," which makes the term "*black quarterback*" sound unusually freakish to me. It's like, a *black* quarterback is an endangered species that inhabits a football field with nine fingers on its throwing hand, eight toes on each of its three feet and a 14-inch Afro stuffed underneath its helmet.

Fritz Pollard, George Taliaferro and Willie Thrower are acknowledged as the first black men to play quarterback for NFL teams. Former Buffalo Bills quarterback James Harris was the first black man to start at quarterback after the AFL-NFL merger in 1970, on Nov. 7, 1971 against the Miami Dolphins. Doug Willams was the first black man to start at quarterback in a Super Bowl—XXII against the Broncos.

"I don't think people thought (blacks) could throw as well or lead as well ... I disproved the negative myths about a black man playing the position."
~Marlin Briscoe

Marlin Briscoe is recognized as the first black man to start a professional football game at quarterback in the American Football League, for the Broncos on October 6, 1968 against the Cincinnati Bengals.

Briscoe was a 14th-round draft choice of the Broncos in 1968. He played collegiately at the University of Nebraska-Omaha. "I thought he was the only guy who could throw the ball then catch his own pass," former pro football star Haven Moses once told me about Briscoe, who finished the '68 season with 14 touchdown passes still a single-season record for Broncos' rookie quarterbacks.

The following season Broncos coach Lou Saban refused to give Briscoe an opportunity to compete for the team's starting quarterback job. In his book titled '*The First Black Quarterback*,' Briscoe chalked up Saban's decision to racial discrimination. The Broncos released Briscoe in '69, and he never started another a game at quarterback in his pro career.

If You Don't Believe Me...

"I got a lot of honors, but my pride and joy is the fact that I was the first black quarterback in the league," Briscoe once told me. "Even though I didn't play quarterback but one year, I think that I proved to the world that a black man could think and throw the football.

"I don't think people thought (blacks) could throw as well or lead as well ... I disproved the negative myths about a black man playing the position."

◆ ◆ ◆

I grew up in an all-black neighborhood on Cleveland's east side. The only white people I recall seeing as a kid were policemen, firemen, our family doctor—Simon Bunin, faculty members at school and, on occasion, those people who read meters for the utility companies.

It was a humorous, innocent act by my youngest sister, Cheryl, that opened my mind to skin tones. Her skin is lighter than mine—yellow to my brown, if you will. Yet, in the eyes of many people, we're both considered "black." Cheryl was two years and eight months old in 1967 when Dr. Martin Luther King Jr. delivered a speech in Cleveland. During the speech Dr. King declared, "*I am black, but I am black and beautiful.*"

I don't know where Cheryl heard Dr. King's words, but she took heed of them—and smeared herself with liquid black shoe dye from the bathroom cabinet. As my mother tells it today, "That girl was gray for days."

A year later, Dr. King was murdered. I was eight years old at the time. News reports showed looting and race-related violence across the country. The manner in which blacks chose to express themselves was confusing—especially after the loss of a man who had persevered through hateful and heinous acts of violence to preach his messages of peace.

But my first personal black-white encounter was anything but violent.

♦ ♦ ♦

Mrs. Hardy was my fourth-grade choir teacher from Parkwood Elementary School. She hosted a "Peace Party" and invited me to her home in Cleveland Heights—the 'burbs. I was 10 years old, and it was the first time I'd been invited to the home of a white family. Just me. No parents or siblings.

I still remember the party invitation—red, with a number of flags representing countries around the world. Momma made sure I was clean and pressed when Mrs. Hardy arrived to pick me up.

It didn't take long for me to realize I wanted to move in with the Hardy family. They had a basketball goal on the garage. My father never would let me have a basketball goal—just a blue scooter he bought for me to ride in circles around the backyard until I couldn't stand up from the dizziness.

Mrs. Hardy introduced me to her son, Henry. We were less than a year apart in age, but Henry was much bigger. We looked like a version of Laurel and Hardy in the backyard—mixing basketball shots with conversation.

I remember that the food was good, we played a game of some sort that involved flags from different countries and I had a new friend, Henry. Not a new *white* friend. Just a new friend. I was glad that Mrs. Hardy asked me to her home and introduced me to her family and friends.

That, and I really wanted Henry's basketball goal.

If You Don't Believe Me...

When I got to junior high school, it was a different game. Margaret Spellacy Junior High, located in a predominantly white neighborhood—as in seemingly 100 percent white. Maybe it was more like 99.8 percent white. My test scores dictated I attend this school, roughly seven miles from my neighborhood. It seemed like 20 miles away because I had to get to and from the school on the stop-and-go city bus route.

There were other blacks who attended Spellacy. They lived closer to the school than I did, but their neighborhood must've seemed further away from mine whenever white kids chased the black kids off the path from the school's front entrance to the bus stop on St. Clair Avenue—which was often.

I thought racism was an adult thing. It wasn't. Some of the kids who laughed and joked with me during class hours stood behind trees and hurled objects while shouting slurs at anyone whose skin tones were dark like mine. At times, we would run into a candy store near the school for shelter. I don't recall the store owner giving out free candy. His protection, however, was plenty sweet.

Eventually, school officials had a bus placed outside Spellacy's front doors, to transport black students and curtail acts of race-related incidents. Those acts which occurred during my junior high years paled in comparison to the ones that took place in senior high school.

◆ ◆ ◆

Collinwood High School. The curriculum was tougher and so was the racism. People sometimes exaggerate about experiences with race. When I'm on stage performing comedy, I joke about them. But it was no laughing matter on a September night in 1974, when one of my classmates was stabbed near the school.

Vincent Brookins was with a group of black students waiting for Collinwood's football team to return from a game. Trouble emerged from the darkness. "We heard these firecrackers go off," Brookins told me in 1998, when I asked him to recall the sequence of events for a column in the News. "After the firecrackers went off, all hell broke loose. White guys came from behind the building, from everywhere with bats, sticks and knives. That really was the first time I had been confronted with that type of situation, the mass hysteria …

"Everybody was running, just trying to get away."

Brookins was confronted by several white males as he sought refuge at a phone booth. One of the men wielded a knife. Brookins told me the nine-inch knife that punctured his heart felt like "a fist to the chest."

"I remember running across the street and almost being hit by a car," Brookins said. "Then I just passed out." Eight hours of open-heart surgery saved Brookins' life. The following week after his stabbing was like no other I've ever experienced in my lifetime. Fights between blacks and whites broke out all over the school. In the street in front of the school, Archie Brookins was stabbed in the back while fighting a group of whites he believed were responsible for his younger brother's stabbing.

Police officers were slow in containing the raging violence. I can recall walking in a dazed state of mind toward the front doors of the school, scared thoughtless from witnessing some of the madness that took place throughout the building — and wondering if I would get home without harm.

During my remaining years at the high school, the racial tensions slowly dissipated. It was almost as if our senior class had made a pact to put the ridiculousness — and life-threatening dangers — of racism to bed for good.

Brookins recovered fully, and went on to become an all-Ohio high school basketball selection. He earned a scholarship at the University of Iowa, where he helped lead the Hawkeyes to the 1980 NCAA men's basketball Final Four. The Detroit Pistons drafted Brookins in 1981, but he didn't make the team and wound up playing professional basketball in Europe. Today, Brookins runs a not-for-profit organization for youths in the Cleveland area. "After the stabbing my mom would tell me I was blessed to do good things because I wasn't supposed to live," Brookins said.

♦ ♦ ♦

Dr. King often called for people to "desegregate" their minds. Washington's words—"*Separate the wheat from the chaff ...* "—came from the Bible's Book of Matthew. Preaching is not my forte and race relations is not my field of expertise. But I would offer that when it comes to judging and discussing the impact of race, be it in sports or other facets of society, one should make a conscious effort to separate the meaningful from the meaningless.

ONE IN PARTICULAR

"The makeup of a successful athlete is difficult for some people to understand. To go beyond logic, the inconceivable, to do what is considered impossible ... that's what makes us tick."

~Sugar Ray Leonard

I enjoy watching team sports. However, I always have been intrigued by the intensity generated from individual competitive sports such as golf, boxing and tennis.

At least 95 percent of the press passes I still possess from two decades worth of events involved team sports. Regrettably, some of the most prestigious individual events in sports history, such as The Masters in golf and Wimbledon in tennis, are missing from my journalist resume.

In August, 2005 I had the pleasure of meeting two of the greatest athletes who ever have competed in individual sports. I shook hands and spoke briefly with golf legend Jack Nicklaus, who holds the record with 18

If You Don't Believe Me...

wins in major tournaments. I spoke by telephone with Chris Evert, who won 18 Grand Slam women's singles titles in tennis. I regret not being afforded more time to listen to stories about their illustrious careers.

Having opportunities to meet and talk with legends is one thing. Attempting to duplicate their athletic abilities, for me, was a whole different story.

♦ ♦ ♦

One summer, I gave tennis a try. I could never get the hang of it—it felt like I was chasing after flies. The flies always were winning and I always was worn out. But I understood the scoring of the game at a very early age, and always have held an appreciation for the talents of the game's top players, past and present.

Now, golf? Blame Tiger Woods for making me believe I would master the game. Never mind his affect on youth all over the world. Woods hit the Professional Golfers' Association Tour as a rookie during the summer of 1996, won The Masters in the spring of 1997 and made it almost mandatory for everyone—no matter what race, creed or color—to know how to play golf.

Guys that I knew who couldn't tell the difference between a 2-iron and a putter suddenly were buying clubs, bags, spikes, polo shirts, tees, course GPS systems and boxes of balls—lots of boxes of balls. Apparently, those same guys were buying lessons, as well, because today they play the game quite good.

I've got golf clubs and all the accessories, too. But my golf score always is higher than my bowling score. In case you're wondering, I'm good for at least 115 any day at the bowling alley.

♦ ♦ ♦

In February 2008, I went to the World Golf Championships' Accenture Match Play event in Marana, Arizona. During the third round, I might have cost Woods a hole during his match against Australian Aaron Baddeley.

SHARING A LAUGH WITH TIGER WOODS IN 2008

My purpose for being at the event was to walk every hole with Woods, then write a column about the experience of watching from up close while the world's greatest golfer was at work. Things were fine for the first 12 holes. Hole No. 13 proved to be unlucky.

While Woods prepared to swing from the hole's elevated tee box, I sought to get ahead of the gallery by walking toward the fairway. Actually it was more of a wander, and I didn't realize anyone—especially not Woods—could see me in a small patch full of cacti.

Woods' caddy at the time, Steve "Crocodile" Williams, yelled loudly in his Aussie accent, "You wanna get outta there mate?" I looked up and saw Woods, Williams and others in the gallery glaring down at me from afar. I ducked out of sight and didn't move until I heard Woods' club hit the ball. His errant tee shot sailed wide to the right of the fairway and hit a marshal in the head.

My photographer for the day, Barry Gutierrez, tended to the wounded volunteer before tournament officials arrived with medical help. Woods stopped by, to offer the marshal an apology and autographed glove.

If I had chosen to follow Gutierrez onto the fairway, Woods' concentration probably wouldn't have been distracted. He probably wouldn't have bloodied a marshal's forehead — and he might not have lost the hole.

Woods regained his composure and beat Baddeley in 20 holes en route to winning the tournament championship. Four months later, he won the U.S. Open while playing with a badly injured knee that required reconstructive surgery after the tournament.

"You kind of think of (fame) as being seductive and a certain lifestyle that you want to be a part of."

~Grant Hill

In November, 2009 Woods' life changed dramatically when he was involved in a car crash and the world learned of his marital infidelities. Woods went through rehabilitation, apologized on national television, became the butt of jokes and let down thousands if not millions of people who, right or wrong, idolized him.

Woods' cloak of invincibility had been removed — on and off the golf course. He still is a headliner at tournaments, but Woods no longer is the dominant golfer on the PGA Tour. His plight brought to mind something NBA star Grant Hill once told me about the perils of fame. Hill had just finished his rookie season with the Detroit Pistons in 1995. We were at a basketball camp run by his former assistant coach at Duke University, Tommy Amaker.

"All your life you have people you look up to and idolize," Hill said. "You kind of think of (fame) as being seductive and a certain lifestyle that you want to be a part of — a lot like the entertainment world. A lot like Hollywood, I guess, because you are entertaining in a way.

"You know, in some ways it is that. But in a lot of ways it's not what you thought it would be. And I guess nothing in life is."

Certainly not for Woods, who still is trying to recover from the self-inflicted blow to his image. His fall from grace was reminiscent of Mike Tyson, the former heavyweight boxing champion whose promising career collapsed under an avalanche of shameful acts outside of the ring.

♦ ♦ ♦

In my comedy act, I playfully refer to having once interviewed Tyson. Truth is, it never happened. I never said to Tyson that he looked like a pit bull but talked like a poodle. If I had done that, a few of my teeth — and maybe one of my ears — might be missing. Tyson assaulted boxing's history books with his devastating punches. I wouldn't dare risk him doing the same to my face.

I tried boxing, but it was another short-lived career move on my life's resume. Two hours, maybe. Once, I went to a gym in Cleveland with my friend, Derek. He preferred to be called by his last name, Gant. First thing the trainer had me do was practice circling inside the ring. I almost puked from dizziness after the first three minutes.

Gant loved boxing. He threw lightning-quick air jabs and had the Ali Shuffle down pat. I never saw anyone hit Gant. Then again, I never saw him hit anyone. I suppose that made Gant undefeated.

If You Don't Believe Me...

Gant also had a knack for talking me into doing things that I shouldn't do. On June 20, 1980 he talked me into going with him to Public Auditorium in downtown Cleveland, to watch the World Boxing Council welterweight championship fight between Sugar Ray Leonard and Roberto Duran on closed-circuit television.

Watching the fight on pay-per-view at home wasn't an option. Neither of us could spare the money to view the fight at the auditorium. Gant wanted to sneak in. I was down with the idea because I liked Leonard and wanted to see him win. I figured the worst that could happen was that we'd fail to find an unlocked door — or get caught by the cops sneaking in and be booted out of the auditorium.

I didn't know Gant's plan involved scaling the mammoth building until we actually started climbing.

It was like a scene from a comedy movie. Two black guys climbing the side of an auditorium, during dusk no less, one reminding the other not to look down while desperately grasping at creases for their hands and feet to cling onto.

I must've looked like Spider-Man. Or Spider-Bro.

We reached an open bathroom window on the second floor. There was a man standing at a urinal when we climbed in. (Note: Nothing stuns a man in midstream at the urinal like the sight of two dudes coming from out of nowhere into a second-floor auditorium bathroom window.)

Duran beat Leonard by unanimous decision that night. I was so mad afterward that I wanted to jump out of that same window.

♦ ♦ ♦

Twenty years later — March 17, 2000 to be precise — I met Leonard at a world lightweight championship boxing match being held at the University of Denver. When you get an opportunity to speak with people you once considered larger-than-life, you want to see them in the "now" but can't help seeing them as they used to be.

Leonard was 43 at the time. He looked—and I'm almost certain he felt—as if he still could go toe-to-toe for 12 rounds with any boxer in the arena, if not the world. In 1997, Leonard announced his fifth and final retirement from pro boxing at age 40.

"The makeup of a successful athlete is difficult for some people to understand," Leonard once told me in an interview for the *Rocky Mountain News*. "To go beyond logic, the inconceivable, to do what is considered impossible ... that's what makes us tick."

In his day, Leonard was an Olympic gold medal winner and professional boxing champion whose good looks and likability afforded him commercial endorsement opportunities. He was like Muhammad Ali Lite—he fought great, but with a third-less braggadocio and controversy.

The public adored Leonard, mainly because it felt as if they knew him both in and out of the ring.

Retired legends like Leonard still command a spotlight in boxing—a sport that has taken a backseat to Mixed Martial Arts and Ultimate Fighting Championship. In particular, boxing lacks the personalities it once had during the sport's heyday. "For me, when I fought we had 'names'" Leonard told me. 'Marvelous' Marvin Hagler. Tommy 'Hit Man' Hearns ...

"You saw us on television. And it was free TV."

◆ ◆ ◆

When I was growing up, you didn't have to be a boxing fan to know the heavyweight champion of the world by name. Ali held the title—and even when he didn't, he talked loud enough to make you believe he still was in possession of the championship belt.

If You Don't Believe Me...

I was introduced to Ali on March 28, 1992, during a small reception in his honor at McNichols Sports Arena after a Denver Nuggets-Phoenix Suns game. We didn't shake hands because Ali was making himself a plate of food. A couple of years later, I bumped into him—literally and physically—while running around the corner of a hotel near Chicago's O'Hare Airport.

In both instances, seeing Ali being beaten down by Parkinson's disease was very hard to handle.

It was Thursday, September 29, 1977 when Ali put his heavyweight championship on the line against Earnie Shavers at Madison Square Garden. I was a freshman at Kent State. The fight was televised nationally, and I watched it with a number of students in our dormitory lounge.

I was a big Ali fan, and he always had the majority of the "People's Vote." Shavers hailed from Warren, Ohio—a town 35 miles east of the Kent State campus. Boisterous shrieks of both amazement and disbelief engulfed the dorm lounge as Ali wobbled badly from Shavers' smashing overhand right in the second round.

Shavers walloped Ali several times through the fight, but Ali was awarded the win with a unanimous 15-round decision. Two years later, Shavers knocked down undefeated champion Larry Holmes, but lost by knockout in the 11th round. It was Shavers' last world title fight.

I met Shavers for lunch at a Denver sports bar in January, 1998. He seemed to be a charming fellow. If you didn't know him, you'd never guess that Shavers was a former boxer who won 68 pro fights by knockout.

Shavers and I laughed often while talking about our Ohio backgrounds. We talked about several of his fights, the wins and the losses. One of his 14 pro losses occurred on September 13, 1975, in a bout against rugged Ron Lyle at Denver Coliseum. Four months earlier Lyle lost a title bout to Ali. Against Shavers, Lyle overcame a second-round knockdown to win the fight by sixth-round knockout.

Many observers—Shavers and his handlers included—believed Lyle, a Denver resident, benefitted from a "hometown" 10-second count, as well as additional time on the corner stool in between rounds. I didn't see the Lyle-Shavers fight. But I did watch Lyle's next fight four months later—a nationally-televised brawl with George Foreman.

> *"Today you get 10 or 20 fights, you fight for the championship. Most of the guys who were around my time had to have a hundred fights before a championship fight."*
>
> ~Jake LaMotta

January 24, 1976. It was Foreman's first fight in 15 months after losing his title to Ali. It was the most exciting fight I'd ever seen—two pure sluggers who found defense to be useless. Lyle dropped Foreman twice in the fourth round, got knocked down once by Foreman in the fourth and was knocked out flat on his face after a barrage of unanswered power punches from Foreman in the fifth.

It was boxing's ultimate slugfest and beat down.

Years later, I walked into a popular Denver sports bar on a Friday night. The doorman asked for my ID, which irritated me slightly because I was in my 30s. I grabbed a beer from the bar, and stood near the entrance of the crowded bar—watching a basketball game on one television and a boxing match on another.

If You Don't Believe Me...

The bouncer leaned across the cigarette machine and asked, "You like boxing?" I answered yes. A brief conversation ensued about the best boxing matches we'd ever seen. I didn't waste any time throwing out the Foreman-Lyle fight. It turned into a rant, with me going on and on about how Lyle should've won the bout.

Specifically, I said, "If Lyle knew how to play some damn defense, he would have won the fight."

The bouncer sneered and introduced himself. His name was Ron Lyle.

◆ ◆ ◆

I've met other characters from pro boxing. The late Hector Camacho fought Duran in 2001 at Denver's Pepsi Center. When the bell rang for Round 1, Duran was 50 years old and cranky. He looked 107 by the end of the fight. And Camacho, ever the clown throughout the promotion of the fight, was 39 years old going on 17.

In 1993, I spent some time with former world middleweight champion Jake LaMotta, when he was "only" 70 years old. LaMotta was 90 on January 4, 2013 when he married Denise Baker—his seventh marriage.

When we spoke at a sports memorabilia signing in '93, LaMotta went off about the number of boxing organizations that existed, making it easy for boxers to claim a championship belt. "There's a champion of Avenue A, a champion of Avenue B, a champion of Avenue C … " he told me. "Today you get 10 or 20 fights, you fight for the championship. Most of the guys who were around my time had to have a hundred fights before a championship fight."

LaMotta made his professional boxing debut in 1941, and won his first world championship in 1949.

His autobiography, "Raging Bull" was released in 1970. That same year, a 21-year-old Foreman won 12 pro fights. On November 5, 1994, Foreman was 45 years old when he became the oldest man to win the heavyweight championship.

♦ ♦ ♦

Foreman's knockout victory over Michael Moorer at the MGM Grand Garden Arena was one of the more amazing events I've ever covered. For nine rounds, Moorer bruised the bigger, slower and older Foreman. In the 10th, Foreman knocked Moorer to the canvas with a three-punch combination. The referee's 10-count seemed to last for an hour. The crowd roars were deafening. I tried to capture the scene around me while keeping track of Moorer. I'd look up and see a celebrity like Magic Johnson standing and staring in disbelief, then look down at Moorer still on the mat struggling to rise to his feet.

Moorer failed to beat the referee's count. When the end of the fight was signaled, Foreman dropped to his knees in a corner and gazed toward the arena ceiling. In the post-fight press conference, I asked Foreman what he could possibly do to surpass his historic achievement that night.

Foreman laughed, then said, "On this planet, we will always know that the athlete of athletes are between the ages 45 and 55. Don't ever let anybody tell you what you can't do. And don't go to Las Vegas and bet against George Foreman."

I strolled around the lobby of the MGM Grand until the wee hours of the morning, clutching beers in both hands while watching gamblers win and lose—and knowing that I had witnessed and written about boxing history.

If You Don't Believe Me...

It was quite a memorable first trip to Las Vegas. I went to bed at 4 a.m. Problem was, in all the excitement I'd forgotten I was responsible for driving to Los Angeles Sunday morning, to cover a Broncos-Rams game that afternoon.

It was one time when help from a teammate—not to mention a few more hours of sleep—sure would have come in handy.

TO FATHERS, WITH GLOVE

"The Hall of Fame is one of my goals. Winning (a World Series) is another. I don't think I'll struggle in the Hall of Fame department. I'm struggling in the winning department."
~Barry Bonds

The Baseball Writers Association of America still sends me a National Baseball Hall of Fame voting ballot, but after the "Great Shutout of 2013" the BBWAA might strip me of the voting privilege.

Why? For starters, I haven't been affiliated with a newspaper for four years. That, and I voted for Barry Bonds and Roger Clemens—two disgraced and despised superstars on the ballot. No players were elected in 2013, which bordered on absurdity considering some of 37 players listed on the ballot—Mark McGwire, Sammy Sosa, Jack Morris, Curt Schilling, Craig Biggio, Mike Piazza, Tim Raines, Lee Smith and Don Mattingly among them.

If You Don't Believe Me...

Each Hall of Fame voter is allowed up to 10 selections. I waited until the last possible moment to mail in my ballot.

◆ ◆ ◆

I also cast votes for Morris and Biggio. At the end of the 2012 baseball season, Morris ranked among Major League Baseball's top 50 in career strikeouts, innings pitched and regular season wins. He went 4-2 in seven World Series starts for three different championship teams. Morris failed to receive enough votes to make the Hall of Fame in 2013.

Biggio ranked 21st on MLB's all-time list with 3,060 hits. He was also fifth all-time with 668 doubles, and was a seven-time All-Star and four-time Gold Glove winner with a lifetime .281 batting average in 20 seasons. He fell 39 votes shy of election into the Hall in 2013.

I did not cast a vote for Sosa or McGwire—long-ball hitting monsters of the "Steroid Era." Their home run totals rank among the top 10 all-time in MLB—Sosa eighth with 609 homers in 18 seasons, McGwire 10th with 583 in 16 seasons. I considered their home run totals before steroid allegations mounted during their record chase in 1998—McGwire had 387 in 13 seasons, Sosa 207 in nine seasons.

I also considered their all-around play. To me, neither Sosa or McGwire was an outstanding fielder—with one Gold Glove awarded between them (to McGwire) in 34 combined seasons of MLB experience.

I voted for Clemens, for the very same reason that I voted for Bonds—Clemens had compiled Hall of Fame-worthy statistics prior to allegations of steroid use. If it's about statistics—and the Hall of Fame vote usually is—Clemens' numbers after 12 seasons compared favorably to Hall of Famer Sandy Koufax. Clemens was 32 years old in

1995 when he completed his 12th season in the majors. He had a 182-98 record, with 36 shutouts and 2,333 strikeouts in 2,532 1/3 innings pitched.

Koufax retired at age 30 after the 1966 season because of arthritis in his pitching (left) elbow. In 12 seasons Koufax won 165 games, threw 40 shutouts and had 2,396 strikeouts in 2,324 1/3 innings pitched.

♦ ♦ ♦

I always have wondered where and when the trail of performance-enhancing drug (PED) use actually began in MLB. I wondered if MLB truly cared about cleaning up its game. The chase in 1998 between McGwire and Sosa to break Roger Maris' single-season home run record (61) pumped much-needed interest into the game. MLB didn't seem to be in much of a hurry to shun the attention—or punish its players who tested positive for PEDs.

Mandatory punishment for positive PED tests in MLB started in 2004. My feeling has been, by waiting so long to punish its players, the league failed to discourage the use of PEDs. Neither the players nor their union were worried about punitive measures. In the meantime, the prodigious and frequent home runs resulted in lucrative new contracts for some players and more fans in the seats at the ballparks.

Once, during a conversation not related to PEDs, Hall of Famer Frank Robinson reminded me, "The fans don't enjoy pitching duels. They enjoy home runs. They enjoy runs scored." McGwire, Sosa and Bonds were league-wide home run-hitting box office superstars. Consider these tidbits, taken from the Web site Baseball-Reference.com— in 1997 only 10 of MLB's 28 teams averaged 30,000 or more fans per game. There were 4,640 home runs hit that season. The following season, teams combined to hit a MLB-record

5,064 homers—and 16 of the league's 30 teams averaged 30,000 or more fans per game. Seventeen MLB teams averaged 30,000 or more fans per game in 2000—when teams combined to hit 5,693 homers.

The jump in attendance, as well as home runs, was hard to overlook in San Francisco. The Giants averaged 23,770 fans per game in 1998. In 2001—the season in which Bonds hit a MLB single-season record 73 home runs—the Giants averaged 40,888 fans per game.

♦ ♦ ♦

> *"The same stinky floors, same tiny lockers and smelly bathrooms. You come here and eat the same sandwiches every day. Somebody puts hot sauce in your pants or something ... It's home, man."*
>
> ~Barry Bonds

In March, 2001 I interviewed Bonds at his locker inside an empty clubhouse at the Giants' spring training facility in Scottsdale, Arizona. The Giants' public relations department made it clear Bonds wasn't doing interviews—and they weren't going out of their way to make me feel special by asking him to do one. Bonds seemed to have a genuine disgust, if not pure hatred, for the media. The only reason I was able to get time with him was because I mentioned the name of a mutual friend we have in Denver.

> *"What somebody did yesterday can't help them today. That's basically how I was taught. Whatever you did yesterday, that doesn't mean anything. That's yesterday. You have to go out and do it today."*
>
> ~Ken Griffey Jr.

"See me tomorrow and I'll do it," Bonds said. On the inside I was feeling jiggy. Outwardly, I maintained a cool look and politely asked, "What time should I be here?" Like a doberman, Bonds snapped, "I said be here *tomorrow*." The next morning, I stopped at McDonald's, picked up a breakfast sandwich and some orange juice, got to the Giants' training complex at 6:30 and sat in the rental car listening to talk radio while waiting for Bonds' arrival.

Bonds arrived less than an hour later. I waited inside the Giants' clubhouse for two more hours before he pulled up a chair and invited me to his locker. By then, most of the team had left the complex for a road game.

At that time, suspicions about Bonds' steroid use hadn't reached a boil. So the conversation for my column in the *Rocky Mountain News* focused on his longevity in the game, his family, not having a World Series ring and reaching the Hall of Fame.

Bonds cited "the same stinky floors, same tiny lockers and smelly bathrooms," as to what lured him back to spring training each year. "You come here and eat the same sandwiches every day," he told me. "Somebody puts hot sauce in your pants or something … It's home, man."

If You Don't Believe Me...

Detractors might point to use of performance-enhancing drugs as the reason for Bonds' prolonged career. When I asked Bonds why he had lasted so long in baseball, he cited genetics and hard work. "If you want to make the Hall of Fame and do things in this game, longevity is the key," he told me. "If you play long enough, good things will happen. The Hall of Fame is one of my goals. Winning (a World Series) is another.

"I don't think I'll struggle in the Hall of Fame department. I'm struggling in the winning department."

If the 2013 vote is an indication, Bonds is going to struggle in the Hall of Fame department. Whispers of steroids use turned into outright screams after he broke McGwire's home run record in '01. The following season he hit fewer homers (46), but was walked 198 times—a MLB record at the time—while leading the majors with a .370 batting average.

The Giants went to the World Series in 2002, losing to the Angels. It was Bonds' only World Series appearance, and he batted .471 with four homers.

◆ ◆ ◆

If Bonds was worried about public perception and allegations about steroid use, it wasn't noticeable during the few times I spent time around him away from the ballpark. I've shared laughs with Bonds, listened to live music with him, heard him tell stories and jokes as if he were auditioning to host *Saturday Night Live*. But my Hall of Fame vote for Bonds had nothing to do with the fact that I'd seen him in a different light away from the baseball park. I simply considered both sides of the coin.

In this case, it was a two-headed coin. Watermelon-head Barry Bonds and Lemon-head Barry Bonds.

The photos don't lie—Bonds' head appears to have grown considerably larger as he's grown older. Many are quick to link it to steroid use. Maybe it's an image created by his baldness. No matter the reason, Bonds' head was bigger in the latter stages of his career.

When I looked at Bonds' statistics before and after 2000, I favored Lemon-head Barry for the Hall of Fame. Lemon-head Barry was once a leadoff hitter for the Pittsburgh Pirates. He was named the National League's Most Valuable Player three times, named to the National League's All-Star team eight times, won eight Gold Gloves and was a seven-time Silver Slugger award winner.

In his first 14 seasons, Lemon-head Barry compiled 2,010 hits, batted in 1,299 runs, scored 1,455 runs, walked 1,430 times, stole 460 bases, hit 445 home runs and batted .288 in 6,976 at-bats. Those numbers compare favorably to the career statistics for former outfielder Andre Dawson, who was elected to the Hall of Fame in 2012.

Dawson had a career .279 batting average, with 2,774 hits, 438 homers, 1,591 runs batted, 1373 runs scored and 314 stolen bases in a 21-year MLB career.

It's the ever-surly Watermelon-head Barry that a large number of players, fans and reporters seemed to loath—not just as a player but as a person. Watermelon-head Barry finished his 22-year career with a MLB-record 762 home runs. Many of the 317 homers Bonds hit from 2000 until his career ended after the 2007 season still are under suspicion because of steroid accusations.

◆ ◆ ◆

When Bonds and I talked during spring training in 2001 he briefly mentioned Ken Griffey Jr., and how the two have been celebrities since birth. Bonds' father, Bobby, played 14 seasons in MLB. Griffey's father, Ken Sr., played

IF YOU DON'T BELIEVE ME...

19 seasons in the majors. The Griffeys were the first father-son combination to play as teammates, with Seattle in 1990.

Like Barry Bonds, Griffey Jr. was constantly under a special spotlight. Unlike Bonds, Griffey's career has not been shadowed by allegations of steroid use. Griffey Jr. likely will go into the Hall of Fame in his first year of ballot eligibility, which is 2016. Had he not missed 75 or more games in five of the 22 seasons he played, Griffey probably would be the third player in MLB history with 700 or more home runs. He was a 13-time All-Star and a 10-time Gold Glove winner.

Griffey seemed almost as gruff as Bonds when it came to dealing with the media. The difference between the two was, even when Bonds smiled it came across as a sneer. Early in his career, Griffey could be snarky with the press, then turn his baseball cap around, smile for the cameras and become "The Kid."

Prime example: the 1998 All-Star Game played at Coors Field. Everyone anticipated a Home Run Derby showdown between Griffey and McGwire—two of baseball's most prolific home run hitters belting balls into Denver's thin air.

Knowing he was a main attraction, Griffey, 28, acted as if he wanted no part of the event. Eventually, he was persuaded to compete, endured some booing from the fans—and then won the contest. A reporter asked Griffey his thoughts about some of the individual records that were being set during the '98 season—including Sosa hitting 20 homers in the month of June.

Griffey's answer was, "What somebody did yesterday can't help them today. That's basically how I was taught. Whatever you did yesterday, that doesn't mean anything. That's yesterday. You have to go out and do it today."

When I saw "The Kid" play for his hometown Cincinnati Reds nine years later, he was a 37-year-old, oft-injured fading star who still was willing to give up his body to make a play. At one point he scaled a wall while chasing a foul ball, which drew rousing cheers from fans at Great American Ballpark.

"I give everything I have, and if I get hurt—there's no ifs," the soft-spoken Griffey told me in the corner of the Reds' clubhouse afterward. "My thing is, you go out and play hard, you'll do more good things than bad. It's the same attitude my dad taught me."

◆ ◆ ◆

During the 1993 season I stood behind a batting cage at Royals Stadium in Kansas City, and watched some playful batting practice banter between a foursome of Royals manager Hal McRae, his son Brian—who played outfield for the Royals, Griffey Jr. and his father, who was the Mariners' batting coach. Seeing them together reminded me of how fathers and sons seem to connect through baseball like no other sport.

When I interviewed Mickey Mantle by telephone for *The Denver Post* in June, 1994, he said he learned at age four how to hit left-handed from his father, Mutt. To this day, Mantle is considered the greatest switch-hitter in MLB history. He won three Most Valuable Player awards during an 18-year career with the New York Yankees, and hit 536 home runs—373 of them from the left-handed batting stance.

"My dad made me start switch-hitting," Mantle told me. "I was a natural right-handed hitter, and I think anyone who is a switch-hitter, their natural stance is their best. It was hard for me at first. I can remember when I was a kid, if my dad wasn't there I'd hit right-handed against everybody."

By the time my brief conversation with Mantle ended, I was feeling like a giddy 10-year-old again. And I felt fortunate to have had an opportunity to speak with him. A year later, Mantle died from cancer at age 63. Ten years earlier my father died from cancer at age 57.

If You Don't Believe Me...

◆ ◆ ◆

I was 10 years old in the summer of 1970 when I got my first baseball glove. My father, Samuel Sr., bought it while our family was on vacation in Covington, Georgia—my parents' hometown. I admit to being guilty of a baseball sin—I cannot remember the make or the player's signature engraved on my first glove.

Before that day, I had only caught rubber balls that ricocheted off the garage in our backyard and left paint chips on the ground as incriminating evidence. I memorized all the wind-up routines for every Cleveland Indians pitcher, then emulated them while throwing the rubber ball off the garage.

Daddy loved baseball. He kept old mitts in the trunk of his car. He liked going to Indians games at Municipal Stadium. More often than not, he left me at home. When he did take me, we didn't talk much. We didn't need to. Just being at the ballpark together spoke volumes to me.

Daddy hands and forearms were very strong. And he had a menacing glare—one I'm sure he used from the mound while playing organized baseball in his teens. When we got into position to play catch, I should have feared the thought of Daddy's throws. But I wasn't scared. I slipped on the glove, happy that I finally would play catch with a real baseball—and with my father.

For a half-hour, Daddy's hard throws into my new glove produced a loud "popping" sound, each throw knocking me out of a catcher's crouch onto the red clay that coated my grandparents' driveway. At one point, Grandma came out of the house and yelled at her eldest son, "*Samuel, stop it—you're hurting that boy!*"

I hollered back, "*No he's not, Grandma!*" I believe that remark got under Daddy's skin. His next throw exploded in my glove. Never mind the gloved hand—the entire right side of my body went numb.

That day, Daddy formally introduced me to the game of baseball. I don't believe I ever bought a baseball glove for my son—which might be the "cardinal" father-son baseball sin.

Major League Baseball, I believe, has many more disgraceful sins of the game to forgive.

◆ ◆ ◆

SWING...AND A MISS AT MILE HIGH STADIUM.

Accounting For Greatness

"You ask any quarterback that has played the game who has achieved and won championships, they will all talk about (courage). That's a characteristic that is common among those."
~Bart Starr

Who is the greatest quarterback of all-time? It's one of the great sports arguments of all-time. For some reason, it's important to have a firm opinion on the subject — whether you're at a sports bar, a coffee shop, a barber shop or cocktail party.

There's a long list of current Hall of Famers to choose from — with Joe Montana, John Elway, Dan Marino, Terry Bradshaw, Roger Staubach, Johnny Unitas, Bart Starr, Fran Tarkenton, Otto Graham, Norm Van Brocklin, Y.A. Tittle, "Slingin'" Sammy Baugh and Sid Luckman among them. There's the "future Hall of Famer" list too, headlined by

Brett Favre, Tom Brady and Peyton Manning, followed by the likes of Drew Brees, Aaron Rodgers, Eli Manning and Ben Roethlisberger—all of whom have at least one Super Bowl championship win.

And then there's the list of 21st century "iEra" stars such as Andrew Luck and Robert Griffin III—who, only one full season into their NFL careers were playing under exceedingly high expectations for greatness.

Whenever the subject arises, I wonder: How does one determine who the greatest quarterback of all time is—and really, why is it that important?

I mean, no one ever argues the question, 'Who is the greatest punter in NFL history?' Because no one cares about punters, or place-kickers or left guards. (The greatest punter, by the way, is former Oakland Raider Ray Guy.) Whoever said beauty is in the eye of the beholder wasn't beholden to zone blocking offensive linemen or nose tackles in the 3-4 defense. Beauty, in football, is about the quarterback.

It's *always* about the quarterback.

◆　◆　◆

I covered the National Football League as a beat reporter for four years—two with *The Denver Post* (1993-94) and the other two for the *Rocky Mountain News* (1996 and 1999). Had I stayed on the beat a few years longer, I might have found my way onto the Pro Football Hall of Fame selection committee. It would've been quite the honor, but I would not have been comfortable about being a part of the process. I don't believe the media alone should be the sole selectors for Hall of Fame inductees.

To say that former players and coaches, and current Hall of Fame members are not included in the selection process would be inaccurate. They are consulted by

If You Don't Believe Me...

members of the media for various input about candidates. But those former players, coaches and Hall of Famers do not get a vote.

I believe there should be a committee of former players and coaches—in the Hall of Fame or not—along with a panel of media members who participate in the selection process. Not that his statistics didn't speak loud enough for the media to notice his worthiness, but who would know better about the legitimacy of a player such as Hall of Fame running back Marcus Allen than someone who played with or against him?

Allen once told me, "Too much power is given to (media), and a lot of those choices are based on the accessibility of a player, or whether he was nice—whether he was kind to me during an interview or walked off during one. Those are the criteria for the Hall of Fame.

"We can say he's a (jerk), but he should be in (the Hall of Fame) because he did his thing on the field."

Elway added, "I don't think anybody knows more about the game of football than the guys that have played or coached it. I don't think the media knows more about the game of football than the players that have played it—and I'm not trying to be (critical) ...

"It's like, Bill Gates knows more about computers than you or I know because that's what he does."

Longevity, statistics and championships won seem to be primary factors in voting for the Pro Football Hall of Fame. However, if your character is flawed, you might have a very hard time entering the hallowed halls of greatness.

Former San Francisco 49ers and Dallas Cowboys star Charles Haley might have a slightly better chance of being enshrined in the Hall of Fame if some of his peers had a vote. Haley finished his career with 100 ½ quarterback sacks and five Pro Bowl selections. He is the only man in NFL history to win five Super Bowl rings during a playing career. He's been a finalist among Hall of Fame candidates four times since becoming eligible in 2005. But he's been called surly and combative, and reported obscene behavior around media and teammates seems to have cast a shadow of doubt on Haley's playing accomplishments.

I asked former NFL quarterback Joe Theismann about the Hall of Fame selection process. He told me, "First, (the voters) have to be willing to admit that they don't know everything—which is difficult."

◆ ◆ ◆

When I was nine years old I thought I knew everything about football. I didn't care about quarterbacks. I believed Cleveland Browns wide receiver Paul Warfield was the greatest professional football player of all time. Period.

(That, and Warfield's teammate, Fair Hooker, owned one of the great names in sports history.)

Warfield was an outstanding football player, one born and bred on football in Ohio. He played high school football in his hometown (Warren, Ohio), was an all-Big 10 selection at Ohio State University and was a first-round pick of the Browns in 1964.

Today, my recollections of Warfield are that he was swift, sure-handed, graceful yet gritty. He wore jersey No. 42 and always seemed to wind up getting the football into the end zone. Warfield had 427 catches—85 for touchdowns—during his 13-year NFL career. He *averaged* 20 yards per catch in 157 regular-season games played. A great player, but now I admit not the greatest football player of all time.

In 1970, the Browns traded Warfield to the Miami Dolphins for a draft choice used to select a quarterback named Mike Phipps. Warfield would play in three straight Super Bowls with the Dolphins (VI, VII and VIII) before defecting to the World Football League for one season. He returned to the Browns for two seasons to complete his stellar career in 1977.

If You Don't Believe Me...

At age nine, I was able to separate good from great on the football field. I didn't need statistics to validate Warfield's greatness.

In 1983, Warfield was inducted into the Pro Football Hall of Fame. Earlier that year, three future great NFL quarterbacks were selected in the first round of the league draft—Elway, Marino and Jim Kelly.

The Denver Broncos traded with the Baltimore Colts to acquire the rights to Elway, who was the first player selected in the '83 draft. The Dolphins, starving for a return to their glory days of the 1970s, selected Marino with the 27th pick overall.

♦ ♦ ♦

At the time Elway and Marino were drafted, there was only a handful of "star" quarterbacks in the league. Most of them were aging. Dan Fouts still was the leader of the San Diego Chargers' offense, but at age 32 he started to become injury prone and missed six games during the '83 season. Theismann was 34 in '83 when he earned the NFL's Most Valuable Player award after quarterbacking the Washington Redskins to Super Bowl XVIII.

The Redskins lost Super Bowl XVIII 38-9 to the then-Los Angeles Raiders. It was the best statistical season ever for 36-year-old Raiders quarterback Jim Plunkett. In San Francisco, the 27-year-old Montana posted the best statistics of his young career. Meanwhile, the Houston Oilers were searching for a solid starter at quarterback. The Oilers opened the '83 season with a pair of quarterbacks—34-year-old Archie Manning and 23-year-old Oliver Luck. As fate would have it, years later, their sons (Peyton and Eli Manning, and Andrew Luck) would go on to become the first players selected overall in their respective NFL draft classes.

Elway, Marino and Kelly were expected to infuse excitement into the league immediately. Kelly, however, chose to start his pro career in the new United States Football

League. The Broncos did reach the playoffs in '83, but Elway struggled as a rookie, and at times was on the bench watching veteran Steve DeBerg. Marino, meanwhile, had an outstanding rookie season. A year later, he led Miami to Super Bowl XIX against Montana and the 49ers. The Dolphins lost 38-16.

In the 15 seasons that followed until his career ended in 1999, Marino never played in another Super Bowl. Elway's impact grew stronger during his fourth season, when he led the Broncos to a thrilling 23-20 overtime win against the Cleveland Browns in the 1986 AFC Championship Game. It's a game that forever will be remembered for "The Drive." A year later, it was "The Fumble" by the Browns that helped Elway reach a second straight Super Bowl. The Broncos lost both Super Bowls, to the New York Giants and Washington Redskins, by a combined score of 81-30.

◆ ◆ ◆

It was Montana who staked his claim to greatness while the young stars climbed toward the top of the mountain. The 49ers won four Super Bowls with Montana—including two in Montana's first four seasons as the team's full-time starting quarterback. Only one other quarterback in the history of the NFL had led his team to four Super Bowl championships—the Steelers' Bradshaw. Even though he was credited for duplicating the feat, Montana had leapfrogged Bradshaw in conversations about the greatest quarterback ever.

I remember asking Bradshaw about judging greatness in quarterbacks—and in particular, if he felt dissed by talk of Montana's greatness. "If I'm around Joe Montana, we're both there and the fans clap louder for him, I'm clapping right along with them," Bradshaw said. "I don't mind not being recognized at all—it doesn't faze me in the least. It's my nature, I guess. It's just not that big a deal.

If You Don't Believe Me...

"But also, I can hold my head up when I walk into a room with a John Unitas or Joe Namath. I can hold my head up pretty high. People say they're better than me. I say, 'That's OK — I've got four rings, thank you very much. And I called my own plays, thank you very much. Nobody else called them — I called them. Thank you very much.' That's how I look at it.

"I really didn't have any bad games the last six years of my (career.) I was having more fun than I ever had. The team needed me more than ever — and I relished in that role. I loved it. And yeah, I look back on it and I go, you know, yeah it would have been nice because I could have probably thrown for another 15,000 yards — 12- to 15,000 yards. That would have put me up there around 40,000 yards. But ... so what? I mean, really, so what?

"Now I just don't care."

Bradshaw's Steelers teams were one of the NFL's Big Four during the 1970s. In addition to Pittsburgh's four championships in four Super Bowl appearances, the Dolphins had two titles in three Super Bowl appearances and the Cowboys won two championships in four Super Bowl appearances. The Minnesota Vikings went 99-43-2 in regular season games during the decade of the 70s, and appeared in four Super Bowls — losing all four.

In the 1990s Kelly had a chance to match Montana and Bradshaw. He led the Bills to four straight Super Bowls. Unforunately, Buffalo lost all four times.

Hearing Bradshaw say he didn't care gave me an initial impression that he was bitter and jealous that Montana had matched his championship achievements. But after giving further thought, it made sense that Bradshaw didn't care. When you accomplish great things, why do you need to be reminded of them? What's done is done. You should be content with your accomplishments.

The more I hear arguments about who is the greatest, the more I realize that no one ever will be right. If it's Super Bowl rings won, Bradshaw and Montana are equals. If it's most Super Bowl appearances, Elway and Brady are equals (five apiece.) Brady won three times, Elway twice.

However, Graham led the Cleveland Browns to six consecutive NFL Championship Game appearances, with three championship wins. He is overlooked often in conversations about the greatest pro quarterback ever. Starr isn't readily mentioned, either. He led the Green Bay Packers to six NFL Championship Game appearances from 1960 to '67. The Packers won five of those championship games — and they won the first two Super Bowls ever played.

◆ ◆ ◆

Many people consider Unitas to be one of the three greatest quarterbacks of all-time. He played on four championsip teams (including Super Bowl V) with the Baltimore Colts during his 18-year playing career. Unitas, who died at age 69 in 2002, threw for 40,239 yards and 290 touchdowns, and attempted 5,186 passes in 211 games.

"To put those numbers up with a (12-game and 14-game) schedule wasn't too bad," Unitas told me in 1994. "Now, they play 16 games — plus the fact they're throwing the football 60 times a game. We threw the football 20, maybe 30 times (per game) at the most."

Starr attempted 3,149 passes in 196 regular-season games played. Luckman, who led the Chicago Bears to four NFL championships during the 1940s, attempted 1,744 passes in his entire 12-year career. In one 96-game stretch for the New England Patriots (2002-07), Brady attempted 3,226 passes.

If You Don't Believe Me...

"You've got coaches calling the plays—got coaches calling the plays in high school, you've got coaches calling plays in college ... and how is the kid supposed to learn anything?"
~Johnny Unitas

Throwing passes in bunches is just one facet of the game that allows a quarterback to shape his greatness. The "old-school" quarterbacks tend to look at different intangibles that don't always appear on a statistics sheet when judging their peers, past and present.

For Unitas, it was a quarterback's capability to run an offense without assistance from coaches on the sideline. What he said to me nearly 20 years ago still holds true in today's game. Very few quarterbacks call their own plays.

"They've taken that aspect of the game away from the player," Unitas said. "But it starts back in (youth leagues). You've got coaches calling the plays—got coaches calling the plays in high school, you've got coaches calling plays in college ... and how is the kid supposed to learn anything?

"It certainly is (a missing ingredient). These guys don't have to think. They don't have to do anything. They sit back there, and the coach sends the play in. Half the time (coach) sends it in late, so he's always hurried at the line of scrimmage ... All of a sudden he looks to the defense, he doesn't know what to do and he calls timeout.

"They probably don't study it. I don't know if they do or not. We always studied our offensive calls. We studied the defenses and how they played. You played percentages an awful lot of the time."

◆ ◆ ◆

In a phone conversation, Starr once told me that courage is what put Montana in a class ahead of most of his peers at quarterback. "You begin with traits that are easy to detect when you've played the position," said Starr, who was inducted into the Pro Football Hall of Fame in 1977. "Those who are able to (see the field) also have a great deal of courage—and that's why they can see the field. They're not concerned with anything that is happening around them. Therefore, their vision is not blurred. It's not distracted. They're not concerned with pressure, with rush, with people near them and thus they're able to focus where they should be—and that's downfield …

"If you can't handle the pressure of that situation, you don't belong in a game at (the NFL) level. That's what it's all about—being able to go in and take your team down whenever you have to."

~Joe Montana

If You Don't Believe Me...

"You ask any quarterback that has played the game who has achieved and won championships, they will all talk about (courage). That's a characteristic that is common among those.

"One of my all-time favorites was John Unitas. Montana is as good as anyone who's ever played. (Troy) Aikman, (Steve) Young and Marino all have the great vision as a result of courage. They stand there in the face of someone bearing down about to hit them right in the sternum. They're going to complete the pass and just take the lick. It never fazes them. You have to admire that."

♦ ♦ ♦

So, who then, is the greatest quarterback who ever played in the National Football League?

Montana always seemed to come up big when championships were on the line. The same could be said for Graham, Starr, Bradshaw, Elway and Unitas, or Luckman, Aikman and Brady. All of them, and so many others, have displayed a remarkable penchant for coolness under duress—especially when trailing in the final two minutes of the game.

"If you can't handle the pressure of that situation, you don't belong in a game at (the NFL) level," Montana once told me. "That's what it's all about—being able to go in and take your team down whenever you have to. Granted, it's not going to happen all the time, and you hate to be in that position. But I think what you'll find is, guys who were able to do things at that point of a game are guys that didn't fear being in that position.

"They didn't relish it, but they don't fear being there. I always tried to treat it like the rest of the game."

Elway's teams won five of the six American Football Conference championship games he played. The sting from losing three Super Bowls early in his career was soothed greatly when he retired after back-to-back wins in Super Bowls XXXII and XXXIII.

Montana led the 49ers to four wins in six National Football Conference championships game appearances. In his first year with Kansas City, Montana led the Chiefs to the 1993 AFC Championship Game. Like Elway, Montana has back-to-back Super Bowl championships. Montana engineered a game-winning touchdown drive late in the fourth quarter to beat the Cincinnati Bengals 20-16 in Super Bowl XXIII. The following season he threw five touchdown passes in a 55-10 blowout win over Elway's Broncos in Super Bowl XXIV.

♦ ♦ ♦

Head-to-head in a league championship setting is my tie-breaker for determining the greatest quarterback of all-time. Eli Manning beat Brady twice. Brees beat Peyton Manning. Aikman beat Kelly twice. Bradshaw beat Staubach twice and Tarkenton once. Joe Namath beat Unitas. Graham beat Van Brocklin. Van Brocklin beat Starr. Starr beat Tittle twice. Luckman and Baugh had championship wins against one another's teams.

Montana beat Marino. Elway beat Favre. Montana beat Elway. So make mine Montana No. 1, with Elway No. 2.

Who's No. 3? To me, you can't go wrong with Unitas. Meanwhile, there are two spots to round out a top five, with seven quarterbacks — Brady, Peyton Manning, Bradshaw, Favre, Marino, Starr and Graham — to choose from.

"It's so difficult to rate players and say who's the greatest ever," Bradshaw told me. "It's done in current times — we talk about the 'right now.' But it's not fair to forget about players like Johnny Unitas. As each decade passes and a new star comes on the scene, it's very easy to forget about those who played before them."

If You Don't Believe Me...

I understood what Bradshaw meant. It's difficult to choose — but still fun to ponder. I believe Montana is the greatest quarterback who ever played in the NFL. I think Lawrence Taylor nudges aside Dick Butkus as the greatest defensive player of all-time. Jerry Rice is the greatest wide receiver the game has ever seen. And pound for pound, Jim Brown is the greatest player to ever play in the NFL.

Care to debate?

GRAMMY AND OSCAR WINNER JAMIE FOXX

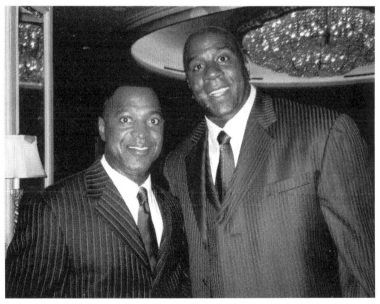

BASKETBALL LEGEND EARVIN "MAGIC" JOHNSON

GRAMMY AWARD WINNER AL JARREAU

COMEDY LEGEND DAVID BRENNER

THE LEGENDARY SPINNERS

MUSIC ICON QUINCY JONES

RUN AND WRITE THE BOLDER BOULDER

CHARLES BARKLEY'S BAG OF TRICKS

My Four Super Bowl "Appearances"

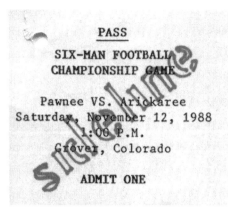

SAMUEL ADAMS
JOURNALIST
SCRIPPS HOWARD NEWS SERVICE

S D
∞ MPC

4

SAMUEL ADAMS
JOURNALIST
DENVER ROCKY MOUNTAIN NEWS

E

0301063-01

INF MPC

4

SUPER BOWL XXXII MVP TERRELL DAVIS

BRONCOS RING OF FAMER ROD SMITH

HALL OF FAMER SHANNON SHARPE MAKES HIS POINT

FOOTBALL LEGEND JIM BROWN

BRONCOS GREAT KARL MECKLENBURG

ANDRES GALARRAGA AKA "BIG CAT"

I Touched the "Cup!"

Holding the Super Bowl Trophy

HALL OF FAMER FLOYD LITTLE

DARRYL DAWKINS AKA CHOCOLATE THUNDER

WAYS OF THE WORLD

STADIUM AUSTRALIA

*"You're a shining star
No matter who you are
Shining bright to see
What you could truly be."*
~Earth, Wind and Fire

What does Earth, Wind and Fire have to do with Olympic relays and performance-enhancing drugs? I will attempt to explain.

When I was a teenager, I played trumpet in a street band named Crosswinds. We performed at bars and cabarets in Cleveland, and got audiences to dance to our covers of songs by Kool and the Gang, KC and the Sunshine Band, Average White Band, the Ohio Players — and just about any other popular funk bands of that time who utilized horn sections.

Earth, Wind and Fire was the hardest band for us to cover. The only Earth, Wind and Fire songs our band played well were "Sing a Song," "Head to the Sky," and "Reasons." Their sound was too perfect to duplicate.

To this day I *adore* Earth, Wind and Fire. Their music if funky and ageless. But a "situation" always seems to arise when I buy tickets to see them perform in concert. Like the first time, back in 1977. I took my best friend's cousin to see the concert. She was 15 years old, but she looked 21. I was 17 but looked 13 years young.

The concert was at Richfield Coliseum — about 40 miles from Cleveland. Earth, Wind and Fire was phenomenal. The "situation" arose afterward. I forgot to take note of where my car was parked. We had to walk around the huge arena parking lot to find my slightly rusted, dark blue 1972 Ford Maverick.

Halfway into the walk, my date bumped into her boyfriend. Man-friend, actually — a bearded dude who, I swear, was dressed like Huggy Bear. You know, the pimp character from the old 'Starsky and Hutch' television series.

The dude gave me a chilling '*Who you supposed to be?*' stare, and then walked off with his girl/woman/my-date-who-is-a cousin-of-my-friend. It took at least another 30 minutes before I found the car. To this day, when I hear the song "Reasons" I wonder why my best friend didn't warn me his cousin had a bearded man-friend Huggy-pimp who also liked Earth, Wind and Fire.

◆ ◆ ◆

If You Don't Believe Me...

There is one other Earth, Wind and Fire "situation" that stands out. I bought a pair of tickets to see the band perform on August 9, 2000 at the famed Red Rocks Amphitheater on the outskirts of Denver. Best seats I'd ever purchased to see the band—within 10 rows of the stage. I had a date, and felt certain she didn't have a Huggy-pimp lurking behind the rocks.

Earth Wind and Fire's lead singer, Philip Bailey, came on stage after a lengthy delay to announce to the crowd that the band couldn't perform due to a malfunction with its soundboard. He promised that the show would be rescheduled. Three weeks later, an announcement was made that show was rescheduled for Sept. 17 and tickets from the August show would be honored.

It was great news—except I wouldn't be dancing in September. At least, not with Earth Wind and Fire. Another "situation" awaited me. On the same day the band announced its new date, I was called into the sports editor's office at the *Rocky Mountain News* and offered an assignment of covering track and field at the Olympic Games in Sydney, Australia.

For me, it was a continuation of a big-time sports writer's roll—having covered four Super Bowls (XXVIII, XXXI, XXXII and XXXIII), an NCAA men's basketball Final Four (1995) and the Major League Baseball All-Star Game (1998)—all within a six-year period.

"*I'm covering the Olympics!*" It sounded cool to say— even though I didn't have a passport.

The reporter who was expected to cover the Games for our paper abruptly took a gig with the rival newspaper in Denver. His cold-blooded move gave me an opportunity I never would have otherwise received. I stepped into his role with wavering confidence.

I knew that my patience, not to mention my versatility as a journalist, would be tested in covering the Games. I had spent several years carving out a niche in the Denver sports scene as a football reporter. Now, I would have to ask questions about the javelin throw, and be accountable for reporting on long jumps, pole vaults and steeplechases—not exactly mainstream sports.

◆ ◆ ◆

My first chore in preparation for covering the Games involved a trip to California, where a number of U.S. Olympians were in final preparations for the Games. I got to spend some time in Pasadena with the women's Olympic swimming team—in particular, previous Olympic gold medal winners Amy Van Dyken and Dara Torres.

Van Dyken reflected on her career accomplishments—which included winning four gold medals at the 1996 Games in Atlanta. She told me she planned to retire after the 2000 Games. It really felt like a tender moment between star athlete and hometown reporter.

"Of course, I retired in 1996, too, and look where I'm at right now," she said, laughing.

"This is bigger than baseball, bigger than the Major Leagues, bigger than the World Series because it's for the United States of America."
~Tommy Lasorda

Then Van Dyken turned serious said, "I honestly believe this is it. I've never said this before. It's really hard because I've been swimming for 21 years (she was

If You Don't Believe Me...

27 years old at the time). Twenty-one years of my life have been spent staring at a black line, hearing coaches yell ...

"And it's hard to say I'm going to retire. I'm leaving swimming, but I'm moving on to other things in my life."

Wow! I had a "scoop" to begin my Olympic coverage. It was easy for other media outlets to laugh it off as common knowledge because everyone assumed that Van Dyken would retire after the Games. After all, at age 31, she'd be too old to compete at the 2004 Games. Right?

No one mentioned age to Torres, who was 33 years old when she made the 2000 Olympic team—her fourth Olympic team. "She took seven years off. Now she's training and swimming like a madwoman," Van Dyken said.

Van Dyken won two more gold medals at the '00 Games, then retired. Torres won five medals in Sydney (and also won three silver medals at the '08 Games in Beijing.)

◆ ◆ ◆

I left the women's swim team in Pasadena and drove to San Diego for the U.S. Olympic baseball team's final media day. The Olympic team's coach was legendary Los Angeles Dodgers manager Tommy Lasorda. Without knowing, Lasorda put my pending Olympic experience into perspective. He told me, "I've managed a world championship team, in World Series and All-Star Games ... To me, (the Olympics) is bigger than all of that. This is bigger than baseball, bigger than the Major Leagues, bigger than the World Series because it's for the United States of America."

> *"You work hard, you fight, you try, you go through injuries, you question your fitness and you question your confidence ... and then you get here in front of the world and you know what you can do."*
>
> ~Jon Drummond

I felt a bit jittery after hearing Lasorda say that it was "for the United States of America." I began to realize I would be at the Olympics writing for an audience far bigger than just readers of the *Rocky Mountain News*. The *world* could be reading my work on the wire services and the Internet.

That's what the Olympics are about. The *world*.

Athletes from all over the world put in countless hours of training, with the intent of performing at the Olympics — where the spirit of competition and sportsmanship are expected to be tantamount, and the pressure to win, for many, borders on overwhelming.

"You work hard, you fight, you try, you go through injuries, you question your fitness and you question your confidence ... and then you get here in front of the world and you know what you can do," U.S. Olympic sprinter Jon Drummond told me.

Knowing what you can do — and actually getting it done on the world's biggest stage for international competition — are two different things.

♦ ♦ ♦

If You Don't Believe Me...

It was because I was on good terms with Ray Crockett — a defensive back on the two-time Super Bowl-winning Denver Broncos teams — that I earned an unofficial gold medal just before the start of the Olympics. Crockett gave me the telephone number for his longtime friend — world champion sprinter Michael Johnson. I conducted an interview with the press-averse Johnson from a pay phone in a concourse at Los Angeles International Airport, minutes before boarding my flight to Sydney.

Johnson, who was 33 years old at the time, told me any expectations for him to top his record-setting gold medal performance at the 1996 Games in Atlanta were outright ridiculous. His goal for the 2000 Games was simple — become the first man to win consecutive Olympic gold medals in the 400-meter dash.

Nothing more. Nothing less.

"I enjoyed '96 because I had a great opportunity to establish my place in history," Johnson told me. "At the same time there was a lot of pressure — pressure I put on myself to do something never done before. So my focus was straight-up business from Day One.

"The difference (in 2000) is, I will not be the major focus, the primary focus, trying to make history. I'm going in already having established my place in history. So I'll be able to enjoy the Olympics as it's happening …

"I understand it's the standard that I have set. But the name of the game is to go out and win. I can't focus on the spectacular with a target already on my back.

"Nobody's happy unless you're spectacular — and that's a risk. If you lose, they say you get what you deserve. I know that my objective is to win a gold medal. Period."

I arrived in Sydney knowing my primary duties would be to cover track and field events. But I did receive a couple of non-track related assignments — including the Olympics' inaugural men's and women's triathlons held at the start of the Games. Running. Swimming. Biking. Three of my least favorite athletic "ings."

The finish lines for the triathlons were at the famed Opera House, which allowed some flavor of Sydney to saturate my soul. Once the track and field competitions started at Stadium Australia, I began to feel the competitive spirit of the Games—along with some feelings of inadequacy as an investigative reporter.

The touchy-feely human interest stories are relatively easy to find at the Olympics. Writing about the outcome of events is easy, too. News outlets, however, crave the behind-the-scenes stories (and rumors) that boil with controversy—especially when the world is watching. When one news outlet is credited for breaking a story that the rest of the world's news outlets have to follow … let's just say it's almost better than sex.

Performance-enhancing drugs were the red-hot topic in Sydney. There were a number of suspected users competing at the Olympics—and plenty of reporters from all over the world on hand searching for incriminating evidence.

I wasn't one of them.

When I accepted the assignment of covering the Olympics, I gave no thought to the possibilities of reporting on PED use. By nature, I'm not a controversy seeker. The whole "Whose performance is enhanced by banned substances?" controversy that accompanied so many events at the Olympics wasn't my thing. Had I made those feelings known to my sports editor, I might never have been allowed to leave Denver for Sydney on the paper's dime.

Controversy festered at the Games. Despite my unwillingness, I had to follow it.

◆ ◆ ◆

If You Don't Believe Me...

World champion shot-putter C.J. Hunter had earned a place on the 2000 U.S. Olympic track and field team. But he withdrew before the Games' opening ceremonies, citing a leg injury. Later, it was learned that Hunter had tested positive for steroids two months before the start of the Olympics.

At the time of the 2000 Olympics, Hunter was married to Marion Jones—the darling of the U.S. women's track team. She arrived in Sydney with an opportunity to win an unprecedented five gold medals.

I was at a non-track event when a U.S. Olympic media official tracked me down by telephone. He urged me to get to Mercure Hotel immediately for a press conference involving Hunter and Jones. There was no transportation available from the venue, so I ran through the streets of Sydney—stopping only once to ask the location of the hotel. Gasping for air, I arrived at the hotel for the start of the press conference—and one of the most bizarre scenarios I ever encountered as a sports reporter.

Jones and Hunter came out together and seated themselves at a table. Famed lawyer Johnnie Cochran was on site, too. So was Victor Conte, whose name later became affixed to performance-enhancing drugs.

"I'm here to support my husband," said Jones, who had won a gold medal in the 100-meter dash two days earlier. Then she abruptly left the room—leaving Hunter alone to sweat in the hot lights of the TV cameras while under a barrage of questions from the press about reports of his positive tests for nandrolone and testosterone.

There already were whispers and suspicions about Jones' possible use of performance-enhancing drugs. In the past, she brushed them aside with ease. After Hunter's publicized test results, Jones, who at the start of the Games had told me, "Fun is winning," found it tougher to laugh off rumors of her PED use as the Olympics wore on.

"People that know me know I'm clean," Jones said during one media session. "Without a doubt, there was pressure coming here saying I wanted to win five (gold) medals." Indeed, Jones left Sydney with five medals — three gold and two bronze. In 2007, the International Olympic Committee stripped her of them after she pleaded guilty to lying to federal investigators about steroid use before the start of the 2000 Olympics.

Jones served a six-month jail sentence that began in March, 2008.

♦ ♦ ♦

STANDING WITH MICHAEL JOHNSON AFTER HIS FINAL OLYMPIC RACE

So many things involving U.S. track athletes were happening away from the field of competition. I went to a press conference called by members of the U.S. men's 4x100 meter relay team. Most of them — including 100-meter Olympic champion Maurice Greene — were represented by H S I, a California-based sports agency. There was some bitterness amongst the relay members that an H S I stablemate, Curtis Johnson, was not selected to the six-man relay pool.

Johnson ran the second-fastest 100 meters at the U.S. Olympic trials, and advanced to the 100-meter semifinals in Sydney. While I felt for Johnson being left out of the relay pool—he said, "To have it taken from you ... it's like losing a family member."—I was turned off by the loyalties some of the sprinters showed to their agency over their country.

An even bigger turnoff was the clown-like celebration of the U.S. team on the medal stand after winning the 4x100 meter relay gold medal. Muscle flexing and tongue-wagging. I found it to be silly, selfish and classless.

Greene anchored the relay team—and was in the middle of the embarrassing acts by the Americans that occurred at the end of the race. He boasted that he'd win gold in Sydney, and he backed up the talk by winning the medals. "You all say I'm very cocky. I'm no different than any other sprinter," Greene said. "I don't think me saying I'm going to win a gold medal offended the others. If you do not believe, you'll have a very hard time (winning.)"

◆ ◆ ◆

Michael Johnson achieved his primary goal by winning a historic second consecutive Olympic gold medal in the 400-meter dash. "I was just pleased and just elated on the podium to be able to stand there knowing that throughout my career I've been able to respond to the pressure," Johnson said after the race. "The pressure was on ... and I was able to respond to it."

I looked forward to having the opportunity to see Johnson anchor the men's 4x400 meter relay team. It would be the final race of his Olympic career.

While I found Johnson to be a bit arrogant at times, he exuded class on the track. He wore gold shoes during races, but Johnson didn't seem accepting to the label of "golden boy" of the Games. He just enjoyed proving he was the best at his craft without rubbing in bravado at the end of the race.

The U.S. 4x400 meter relay team of Johnson, twins Alvin and Calvin Harrison and Antonio Pettigrew won the gold medal easily. Afterward, Johnson took a farewell lap around the stadium track.

"I've gotten to the point where there's nothing to be gained by running another world championship," Johnson said. "I think I've gotten to the point right now where the risk is greater than the reward. I still love competing, but the risk of going out there and messing up what I've been able to build up over the last 10 years is just too great. It's just not worth it."

I was reminded of Johnson's words when, in August 2008 Pettigrew admitted to using PEDs at the 2000 Olympics — thus disqualifying the 4x400 meter relay team's gold medal-winning efforts. All six members of the relay pool — including Johnson — returned their medals to the International Olympic Committee. Two years later, law officials in Chatham County North Carolina found Pettigrew inside his car, dead from an apparent suicide.

◆ ◆ ◆

When I returned to Denver from the Games I received an e-mail from Barry Forbis. He is the sports editor who chose me to travel to Sydney, when all I really wanted to do in September was watch Earth, Wind and Fire perform at Red Rocks and see the Broncos start their season.

> "Sam, I can't express how much I appreciate the work you did before and during the Sydney Olympics. When (we were left) high and dry — and with no stories written for the special section — I was, frankly, a little worried. You pulled that one out for us, and you did a great job in Sydney, too. Every time I talked to you, I seemed to be facing a deadline situation, so let me say it now: You did a first-rate job reporting on track, especially, but also

If You Don't Believe Me...

pursuing other stories we wanted down there—from Michael Johnson to the relay team to Amy and the Golden Girls before the Games and on and on.

"*I know you're tired. Take some time off, and we'll see you when you get back.*"

I waited until the end of the year to make my "Getaway"—to Las Vegas. I watched the Broncos lose a playoff game against the Baltimore Ravens on television at a casino before dealing with a "situation" a few hours later. I had to pick up a free concert ticket left in my name by the band performing at House of Blues.

Earth, Wind and Fire rocked the house.

That "Saturday Nite," I felt like a "Shining Star."

Basketball Jones

"I know North Carolina basketball will keep going long after I'm gone. I hope we win. I hope we play well—and generally that means winning. But I hope I'm not ever taking myself too seriously."
~Coach Dean Smith

Growing up, baseball was the game I played for enjoyment. For some reason basketball brought out a way-too-serious competitor from within me.

Truth is, I never really had much of a game when it came to playing basketball. I frustrated opponents using a combination of long arms and a pretty high vertical leap. On a good day, I was an average player on offense, but one who was real good at blocking shots and stealing passes all day long on defense.

For the record, I still could dunk a basketball when I was 43 years old. I'm not referring to one of those knee-high Nerf ball hoops for toddlers. On a 10-foot high, regulation-sized goal, I could jump up and stuff a regulation-sized basketball into the hoop.

If You Don't Believe Me...

Personally, I think that's a pretty cool athletic feat for a 6-foot tall baby-boomer.

But 2003 was a *long* time ago.

◆ ◆ ◆

I like to believe I learned plenty about basketball from watching Boston Celtics great Bill Russell. He was my first "favorite player" in basketball. It seemed like Russell grabbed every rebound, blocked every shot and his Celtics won every National Basketball Association championship.

I wasn't a Celtics fan, but I dug Bill Russell's game.

Then came Kareem Abdul-Jabbar. He won championships at UCLA and was a superstar rookie with the Milwaukee Bucks. He looked like a giraffe towering over everyone on the court. I loved to emulate his "Sky Hook" shot—and the way he ran up the court with thumbs-up on both hands after scoring. Russell retired at the end of the 1968-69 NBA season. Abdul-Jabbar was a rookie in the 1969-70 season. He became my new favorite player.

Then it was Sidney Wicks—a former teammate of Abdul-Jabbar at UCLA. I liked Wicks' game, but liked the dude's Afro even more. I cut out Wicks' picture from a newspaper article and kept it on my mirror for weeks. He had become my new "favorite player" by a few hairs, until I read a story in *Sport* magazine about a guy called "Dr. J." His real name was Julius Erving.

"I didn't have a ticket.
But I did have a plan.
This was the dumbest
plan I'd ever concocted."
~Sam Adams

The more I saw of Erving in magazines and newspapers, the more I fell in "basketball love." Erving appeared to be walking on air in every action photograph—his right arm stretched high while he squeezed the grip on a basketball that looked more like a plum in his massive hand. And his Afro looked bigger and better than Wicks.

Erving averaged 29 points per game over a five-season span with the New York Nets in the American Basketball Association. He joined the NBA's Philadelphia 76ers in 1976 and immediately became the most interesting, if not exciting player in the league.

Erving was "The Doctor." And he was more than my new favorite player. He had become my idol.

Without knowing so, "The Doctor" helped teach me a most valuable lesson about media etiquette. It came on a night when my career in journalism nearly ended before it ever started.

On December 30, 1986, the Denver Nuggets hosted the Philadelphia 76ers. Erving had announced that the '86-'87 season was the last of his career, so it was going to be his last regular-season appearance in Denver. It would be my last opportunity to see my idol perform in person, and the game was sold out.

I didn't have a ticket. But I did have a plan. This was the dumbest plan I'd ever concocted.

I called the Nuggets' media relations office to request a press pass for the game. I told them *The Denver Post* had assigned me to write about the game. I was told the request would be handled.

Bill Young, who authorized media credential distribution for the Nuggets, handled things by calling Tom Patterson, who was the Post's sports editor. Patterson had no idea I existed. Once he found out I was a neophyte high school stringer, he asked the Post's prep sports editor, Taylor Scott, to call me.

IF YOU DON'T BELIEVE ME...

```
DN1230        Denver Nuggets
SIDE          NATIONAL BASKETBALL ASSOCIATION
LOGE                        VS.
ADMIT1        PHILADELPHIA 76ERS
ADVWIN        McNICHOLS SPORTS ARENA
  18.00       TUE DEC 30, 1986 7:30 PM
PRICE
BOX  1.64     SIDE LOGE          ADMIT
TAX                              ADMISSION
123086      60    I      10         18.00
           SEC   ROW    SEAT    TAX INCLUDED
```

Scott asked me to come to the building. When I arrived, he told me the scheme had been busted. He told me "don't lie" to Patterson.

Patterson was very cordial for all of about 90 seconds before asking if I had called the Nuggets' offices looking for a press pass. I answered yes and explained why. Patterson seemed both understanding and amused by my efforts. He also gave a brief but stern lecture on the ramifications of lying to gain entry into professional sporting events.

Then Patterson opened his desk drawer and offered to sell me a ticket to the game. Section 60, row I, seat 10. It cost me $18 but I bought it and got to see my idol "Dr. J" play his last game in Denver. Erving scored 17 points and the Sixers won. I never asked for a press pass with a purpose of sneaking into a game again.

At the same time that Erving's Hall of Fame basketball career was nearing its end, my career as a reporter (sneaky moments aside) was just beginning at the high school ranks. I paid dues, covering prep events at the lowest classifications while gaining valuable experience.

◆ ◆ ◆

About the same time I started moving up the ladder covering prep sports, there was a kid named Chauncey Billups in Denver's Park Hill neighborhood who was turning heads on the basketball court. Anyone who saw Billups play came away believing that he'd be the biggest hoops star to ever come out of the Mile High City.

Once, I overheard some men in a bar having a "who's-better-than-who" argument about basketball. I didn't know them, and kept some distance while eavesdropping. I was sure the argument was about point guards. Los Angeles Lakers star Earvin "Magic" Johnson, or maybe Utah Jazz point guard John Stockton.

Curiosity got the best of me, so I asked, "Who are you guys talking about?" One of the men turned to me and said, "We're talking about 'Smooth' — Chauncey Billups." These were grown men arguing, over beers, about Billups — who was in middle school at the time.

I still remember Billups' first varsity game. Dec. 3, 1991. I was the only reporter at the game. Billups was a freshman and he scored 17 points playing for George Washington High School, which won the game 67-51.

Billups became a high school All-American, collegiate All-American at the University of Colorado, a first-round NBA draft choice (third overall by the Celtics in 1997), a five-time NBA All-Star and, in his crowning moment as a professional, the Most Valuable Player of the 2004 NBA Finals in leading the Detroit Pistons to the league championship over the Los Angeles Lakers.

What I've come to admire most about Billups over the years is his involvement with local and national charities, as well as his willingness to mentor youth. At times, he'll go out of his way to do so. It doesn't matter if it's an up-and-coming basketball player living in the inner-city, or a rising star golfer who lives in the suburbs.

"For me, I like to do that because that's something I didn't have," Billups told me in an interview with *Colorado AvidGolfer* magazine. "I didn't have anybody to help me or show me how to be, or how to act or how to carry myself … I didn't have that because I didn't know anybody that had done the things that I was doing."

When I watched Billups play throughout his high school career, I felt he would make it to the NBA—but not without some experience playing at the collegiate level. I saw Kobe Bryant play once at the prep level, at the 1996 McDonald's High School All-America Game at Civic Arena in Pittsburgh. By game's end, I *knew* he was ready for the pros.

♦   ♦   ♦

Bryant offered crowd-pleasing glimpses of his well-hyped offensive skills, with break-away dunks and fancy layups. Talking with him briefly at mid-court after the game, I sensed that the confident 17-year-old kid loved to play basketball and mind games.

What better mind game to play. Bryant had college coaches drooling to sign him. And he had NBA scouts guessing—some second-guessing—whether to draft him.

"It's a cool situation to have," Bryant said when I asked him about choosing between college and entering the NBA draft. "If I allow myself to be pressured into making an early decision, the decision might not be for the best."

Bryant's father, Joe, stood nearby. When his son was born in 1978, Joe Bryant was a teammate of Erving with the 76ers.

"He's always been a very creative young man," Joe Bryant said. "I saw him jump off a gymnastic springboard to propel himself for a reverse dunk when he was eight years old. That's when I knew he'd be special … different, whether it was basketball, baseball, football, soccer or whatever."

Bryant needed to mature, more so physically than mentally, to play immediately in the pros. He was well-aware of other players who skipped college to enter the draft—players like Moses Malone, Darryl Dawkins, Bill Willoughby and Kevin Garnett, all of whom were 6-foot-8 or taller.

"I'm a little fella," Bryant told me. "I understand it'll be some adjustments if I did try to make the jump."

Bryant jumped, all right, from Lower Merion (PA) High School to the Lakers. At the beginning of the 2012-13 NBA season he was a 34-year-old, five-time NBA champion who, in his 17th season would become the fifth player in league history to reach the 30,000-point plateau.

For selfish reasons, I wanted Bryant to play college basketball. At the time he was weighing his options, Duke and North Carolina were high on Bryant's list of colleges.

♦ ♦ ♦

In January 1995, I left the Post to accept a job with *The Charlotte Observer*. At the time, I covered the Denver Broncos and NFL beat for the Post. But I coveted the NBA beat. I never felt in awe or nervous around the players—except for the time I almost stepped on Michael Jordan's bare foot before a game— and watched the game with a much different perspective than I did when covering other sports.

It might sound weird, but often times, I would put myself into the body of a player. I was in my mid-30s and still a bit athletic, which gave what I believed to be a better sense for gauging player movement and timing. Often times, I would notice things during the course of a game that led me to ask questions afterward, questions that would lead players or coaches to ask me, "You saw that?"

I tried using my want of covering the NBA as leverage when deciding whether to leave Denver. I received promises from the Post, but I wanted assurances. I didn't get those assurances and chose to accept the job with The Observer.

IF YOU DON'T BELIEVE ME...

◆ ◆ ◆

The opportunity to cover college basketball in the Atlantic Coast Conference, I felt, was too good to pass up. The ACC was considered "NBA Jr." in some circles. So many great NBA players had come out of the ACC over the years. When I arrived in '95, there were future NBA first-rounders on every ACC team roster, the likes of Jerry Stackhouse and Rasheed Wallace at North Carolina, and Maryland's Joe Smith—who would be the first player selected overall in the '95 NBA draft.

I saw Tim Duncan develop into an All-America player at Wake Forest, and watched freshmen Vince Carter, Antawn Jamison and Stephon Marbury take over the ACC as freshmen in 1996. I lived in Raleigh and watched plenty of games at North Carolina State—where the late Jim Valvano's presence still could be felt at Reynolds Coliseum.

Nothing excited me more about covering the ACC than the Duke-North Carolina rivalry. To me it was the best rivalry in basketball, if not all of sports.

◆ ◆ ◆

"The easiest thing to say at that point was, 'Well if coach was there, we would have won,' instead of saying, 'If I rebounded one shot...'"
~Coach Mike Krzyzewski

Tar Heels vs. Blue Devils. With their powder blue uniforms, the Heels seemed to represent something heavenly in Chapel Hill. Duke's reputation was summarized in a word: arrogant. In particular, I looked forward to spending time around the coaches—UNC's Dean Smith and Duke's Mike Krzyzewski. I didn't look forward to having to spell Krzyzewski's name repeatedly while reporting on deadline, but I did look forward to watching him work on the sideline.

Unfortunately, I had to wait for that chance. I arrived in North Carolina on Jan. 8—a day after Duke played its first game without Krzyzewski, who had announced he was taking off for the remainder of the season due to health concerns.

The Blue Devils without "Coach K" were scrappy but beatable, losing 15 of 19 games without him on the bench and finishing 13-18 for the season. Krzyzewski didn't like the perception that things would have gone differently had he been on the bench for those 19 games.

"It was so overriding that it was tough to say how much of a percentage was based on anything," Krzyzewski said during a media gathering in 1996. "If we would have won a couple of games right away, I think it would have been defused. It would have, there's no question about it. It became bigger because we lost—and we lost eight or nine games by such small margins.

"The easiest thing to say at that point was, 'Well if coach was there, we would have won,' instead of saying, 'If I rebounded one shot …' The focus was not on the right thing, and as a result, my absence was made bigger and more important than what it really was.

"They were doing a pretty good job, and then the result was that we didn't win. They played hard and didn't win."

Eight of Duke's losses without Krzyzewski came by six points or less. One of those eight games was played against arch-rival North Carolina on Feb. 2, 1995 at Cameron Indoor Stadium.

If You Don't Believe Me...

It was the best basketball game I've ever witnessed in person.

Duke's home court ought to be called Cameron Indoor Oven. It feels like 450 degrees inside the gym, which crams 9,314 fans for every game. Things might be different today, but at that time, press row was separated from the first row of seats by about a Munchkin's arm length.

Duke's Jeff Capel hit a three-point shot to send the game into a second overtime, and the Cameron Crazies' delirium could be felt, literally, on press row. Fans toppled one another to celebrate. One fan was pushing so hard that my chest was pinned against the press table. I couldn't breathe, and shot an elbow to get the kid off my back.

The Tar Heels, with Stackhouse and Wallace on the floor, were too resourceful and won 102-100 in double overtime. Afterward, coach Smith came into the press room. I was seated close enough to see beads of sweat dripping from his neckline hairs onto the back of his shirt collar. He said, "If you didn't like that, you don't like college basketball."

I loved it. It was exactly the kind of game I wanted to see when I took the job. And I had only one obligatory mention of Mike Krzyzewski to type while on an extremely tight deadline.

It seemed as if Smith had spent his entire life in North Carolina, but he was born in Kansas and played basketball and baseball at the University of Kansas. In the mid-1950s, he actually spent time in Colorado. He was an assistant basketball coach at Air Force Academy, as well as coach of the academy's baseball and golf teams.

My sense was that Smith didn't care for the god-like treatment he received from fans and media at North Carolina. During the NCAA Tournament's Southeast regional finals played at Birmingham, Alabama in 1995, Smith was asked why he never seemed too uptight despite the high expectations for his teams to win year after year.

"I know there are more important things in the world—there's poverty to deal with, and all the killings and violence," Smith said. "I try very hard for our teams to be ready to play. I hope we win. I hope we play well—and generally that means winning. But I hope I'm not ever taking myself too seriously.

"I know North Carolina basketball will keep going long after I'm gone."

North Carolina won the Southeast region and advanced to the Final Four played at the Seattle Kingdome. The Tar Heels were matched against Arkansas, and Smith was asked about having concerns with how the game might be officiated.

Instead of a simple "No" Smith offered the following: "Basketball is a difficult game to officiate, but (the rulebook) still says if I'm shooting or passing and they hit my arm and I have the ball, it's a foul. It's still in the rulebook and you still expect it to be called. I'm amazed at how people say 'how it's called' as if it should be called differently. It's supposed to be uniformed throughout the country …

"I'm driving 70 miles per hour and the other guy is going 90, maybe both of us should be penalized. But the guy who's doing 90, if it isn't called, is going to win the race."

Arkansas beat North Carolina in the semis, then lost to UCLA in the '95 NCAA national championship game. The Bruins were worthy champions. Earlier in the year, I'd seen them pummel Duke at UCLA's fabled Pauley Pavilion—the same college arena where so many Bruins greats had played for legendary coach John Wooden.

♦ ♦ ♦

As much as I liked covering ACC basketball, I missed living in Denver a lot more. The *Rocky Mountain News* had an opening for an NFL beat writer in the summer of 1996, and I was the right person to take the job.

IF YOU DON'T BELIEVE ME...

Coming back to Denver afforded me the chance to see Billups play at Colorado a few times more before he entered the NBA draft. It gave me an opportunity to see him play for the hometown Nuggets during his pro career. It gave me a chance to watch Billups become a man, a husband and a father, while mastering his craft at the highest level.

Whenever I see Billups, I'm still reminded of that 15-year-old freshman phenom I saw sliding around on a slippery high school gym floor while playing his first varsity game. Maybe he remembers seeing me dunk a basketball once at a local health club.

I was 43.

It was a *long* time ago.

9

LOCATION LOCATION

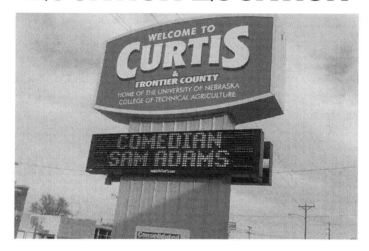

"Knowing that you're obsessed with something doesn't mean it's going to automatically happen."

~Ray Bourque

Nebraska's state slogan is " ... The Good Life." If not for Nebraska, my state of mind probably would be in a state of disarray.

In 2009, I won at the Great American Comedy Festival, which is held in Norfolk, Nebraska—childhood hometown of Johnny Carson. It was the event that fueled my passion to make a living as a stand-up comedian. Since the contest, I've worked more than 40 times in at least 30 towns in

If You Don't Believe Me...

Nebraska. I have posed for a picture with the Nebraska governor in Kimball, had my photo printed on the front page of the *McCook Daily Gazette* (next to a headline that read, "Children allegedly locked in kennel") and even brought home a giraffe leg bone as a "gift" from an overzealous outdoorsman in Sidney.

I first took a liking to Nebraska on November 23, 2001, when I chose to write a column about watching the Nebraska-Colorado college football game at a bar with Cornhuskers fans. Not just a bar. It was The Bar, a watering hole in a town named Hershey. As I like to tell my comedy audiences, the town's name is Hershey, but I don't believe the town's people had ever seen a chocolate-skinned man in person until I showed up.

The people at The Bar chanted "Go … Big … Red" all afternoon long. But Colorado won the game 62-36. I felt fortunate to leave the place in one piece. Since that first trip, I've been back to The Bar in Hershey many times. I enjoy being with the people—and apparently, I enjoy being caught up in unusual situations.

During my time spent as a sports writer, I found myself in unusually weird interview settings on more than a few occasions. Sure, it would be awesome to do interviews from a cushy, intimate stage setting like Oprah or Letterman. Sometimes, it's a matter of where you are at the time—and how far you are willing to go to connect with someone for an interview.

◆ ◆ ◆

I was in Cleveland in June 1994, sitting in my mother's kitchen and trying to negotiate an interview with baseball Hall of Famer Mickey Mantle. At the time, *The Denver Post* had me on assignment to interview Indians player Eddie Murray, for a feature story about baseball's best switch-hitters. Mantle was on a short tour to promote his new book, "*All My Octobers.*" His agent told me the only opportunity I'd have for an interview would be to fly to San Francisco before week's end. When I explained to the agent that I couldn't travel to San Francisco on short notice, she hung up the phone.

The agent did have one slip of the tongue—telling me that Mantle would be in Boston for interviews the following day. With the help of a reporter in Boston, I learned where Mantle was staying and called his hotel room at 7:45 the next morning. When he answered the phone, I introduced myself and told him what I wanted to talk about—while speaking at 100 miles per hour.

There was brief silence before Mantle asked, "How'd you get my number?" I didn't give up my source, but I assured Mantle that I only wanted a few minutes of his time to talk about switch-hitting. "You want to talk about switch-hitting? I'll talk to you about switch-hitting. But I've got to make it quick 'cause I've got an interview in a few minutes."

Mantle gave me 10 minutes of time to talk about switch-hitting. Momma's kitchen was my new hot spot for conducting interviews.

♦ ♦ ♦

"You know that nothing is a given. You play for so long and there (are) no promises. There's no mystery about it—it's nothing but a business so you have to look at it that way."

~Ken Lanier

If You Don't Believe Me...

I've pulled off the road several times to conduct interviews on the phone. Hall of Famers Joe Namath and Bob Griese come to mind. But the situation that takes the cake, for me, was when I interviewed 290-pound National Football League offensive lineman Ken Lanier. Weirdest interview setting ever.

Lanier wasn't a heavyweight on the name-dropping scale. But he had a productive pro football career, having played 14 years in the NFL — the first 12 with the Denver Broncos. In 1993, he signed a free agent contract with the division-rival L.A. Raiders.

When the Raiders visited Denver for a *Monday Night Football* game during the '93 season, my assignment from the Post was to interview Lanier and get his thoughts on playing against his former team for the first time. The Raiders' public relations department offered no help in the interview set-up process. So I pursued Lanier on my own by tracking him down when the team arrived at its hotel in Denver.

Lanier was polite but unreceptive to an interview. But he needed a ride to the airport, to pick up a rental car so he could visit with family and friends in Denver. I offered the ride in exchange for the interview. We made a deal.

The Raiders' hotel was less than 10 minutes from Stapleton Airport. I managed to squeeze 15 minutes out of Lanier, starting from the moment he stuffed his big body into my car — a 1986 Dodge Aries K. I placed a tape recorder on top of the dashboard and asked questions. Lanier, nicknamed "Big Dog," watched the recorder slide across the dashboard repeatedly and wondered how long my car's suspension system would hold his weight.

What Lanier said to me that night about having to find a new team is useful today for people who have been put in a position to find new careers — as I was in '09.

"In the back of my mind—and it should be in everybody's mind—you know that nothing is a given," he said. "You play for so long and there (are) no promises. There's no mystery about it—it's nothing but a business so you have to look at it that way.

"If you start thinking about it another way, it won't work."

♦ ♦ ♦

Two months before I crammed Lanier into my car, I had a conversation with pitching great Nolan Ryan in Arlington, Texas. It would have been nice to sit in front of his locker, but Ryan waved me out to the back of the Rangers' clubhouse, to an area littered with playground toys for the children and grandchildren of the team's players and coaches.

We talked fastballs and sliders while sitting near a teeter-totter and sliding board. Actually, my knees were wedged into a toddler-sized picnic bench when Ryan came outside clutching a bowl of grapes. The interview lasted nearly 45 minutes.

Ryan was near the end of his 27th and final season in the majors. He was 46 years old and struggling with nagging injuries. I was six years old when Ryan made his Major League Baseball debut in 1966. In 1989—at age 42—Ryan struck out 301 batters for the Texas Rangers. Only two American League pitchers have reached the 300-strikeout plateau since—Randy Johnson (308 in 1993) and Pedro Martinez (313 in 1999).

Ryan finished his Hall of Fame career with a record 5,714 strikeouts, 324 wins and a record seven no-hitters— four with the California Angels, one with the Houston Astros and two with the Rangers.

"The only thing I really wanted to do was put four years in the big leagues to qualify for the pension," Ryan told me. "And that was my goal, to qualify for the pension. At that time, it was about the only security I could get out of the game."

If You Don't Believe Me...

He looked fit enough to pitch until age 50, but Ryan had grown tired of being under the media microscope. "I don't know if I'd play anymore even if I could stay healthy, because of all the things that go with the job now," he said. "The demands, the criticism, the scrutiny you're under. It's just that you don't have any time to yourself. Those things have taken away from the enjoyment of the game."

A pitcher with Ryan's combination of durability and capabilities is hard to find these days—and would be worth mega-millions on the MLB market. His record for career strikeouts probably will stand for many years to come. "I don't think we'll see pitchers or players playing that long any more," Ryan said. "They're going to have to stay (in the league) a while."

After the interview with Ryan, I sought shade in the Rangers' dugout while their opponent that night, the Baltimore Orioles, took batting practice in the heat. A man walked into the dugout and took a seat next to me. "Haven't seen you here before," he said. I introduced myself as a writer from Denver. The man said, "I love Denver," talked some about having family in the city and then slapped me on my knee. Hard. I turned, and gave a 'don't-ever-do-that-again' look to the Rangers' Managing General Partner—and future United States President— George W. Bush.

◆ ◆ ◆

Ryan in Kiddieland and Lanier in a K car were unusual interviews settings, for sure. Sometimes, I met famous people in unlikely places with no interviews intended. Like the night I met famed lawyer Johnnie Cochran at the 2000 Olympics in Sydney, Australia, while waiting for a train to ride into the city after a night of reporting on track and field. I spotted Cochran at the station and introduced myself. I had seen him earlier in the week, at a press conference involving U.S. track athletes C.J. Hunter and Marion Jones.

The train arrived, we boarded and I was ready to move on. But Cochran urged me to sit with him. I did, and we started a conversation about football, as well as a mutual friend in Denver — well-known football agent C. Lamont Smith. Meanwhile, word spread that Cochran was on the train. Passengers of different nationalities walked up to our seats to snap photographs. Neither of us could make out much of what the foreign gawkers were saying, except for his name, "*Joh-knee Cock-cran*." Cochran pulled me into the frame every time someone snapped a photo.

Cochran and I exited the train at Circular Quay — the Sydney Opera House stop. We walked in the same direction — Cochran to his hotel, me to a night club near the hotel. As we passed by the Opera House, Cochran wondered aloud if Detroit Lions great Barry Sanders — one of Smith's clients — might consider ending his retirement. I used the moment to bring another retired running back into the conversation. When I asked Cochran if he minded talking about his client, O.J. Simpson, he looked at me with a slight smile, shook my hand, wished me luck in future endeavors and walked into his hotel.

Somewhere in the world there are people with photographs of the late Johnnie Cochran (he died at age 67 in 2005) — with no clue who the other guy is in the picture. But I'm good with that.

♦ ♦ ♦

One time, I posed for a photograph with hockey Hall of Famer Raymond Bourque while we stood in a shower.

A week before the start of the 2001 Stanley Cup playoffs, I sat with Bourque in the Colorado Avalanche's locker room after the team's practice session. We weren't "great friends," but Bourque seemed comfortable with expressing to me his obsession to finally win a championship in his 22nd season playing in the National Hockey League. "It's an obsession … in a lot of ways," he told me for a front-page story which ran in the *Rocky Mountain News*. "It is because that's what's left for me, you know? But knowing that you're obsessed with something doesn't mean it's going to automatically happen."

I've never forgotten those words from Bourque. Or the words John Elway said to me when I asked him to describe one's quest to win his first championship toward the end of a long playing career. Elway knew what Bourque was feeling. He won his first Super Bowl in his 15th season in the NFL. "Everyone says this guy or that guy deserves to win a championship," Elway told me. "I mean, nobody *deserves* it … you have to be in the right place at the right time."

"Going out there and continuing to do what I do, what I like to think that I can do at the same level that I've always been doing it at. That's easier said than done."

~Randy Johnson

Bourque was driven to win a championship, and he expected to be a major contributor in the Avalanche's run to the Stanley Cup Finals. At age 40, he was slowing down, but Bourque hadn't lost an ounce of his competitive edge. He still was one of the best defensemen in the NHL, and his slap-shot was every bit as lethal as a Randy Johnson fastball.

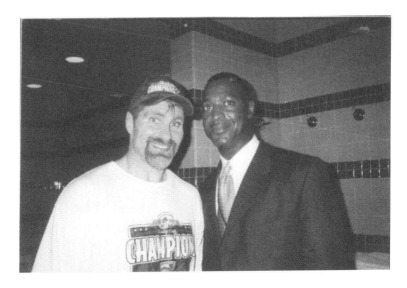

Johnson, who ranks second to Ryan on MLB's all-time strikeout list with 4,875, also could identify with Bourque's obsession. He reached his first World Series in his 14th season. After a spring training game, I asked Johnson what kept him motivated to play. "Being competitive," he told me. "Going out there and continuing to do what I do, what I like to think that I can do at the same level that I've always been doing it at.

"That's easier said than done."

Winning the first championship was much easier said than done for Bourque. But I felt confident that he would hoist the NHL's championship trophy—even when the Avs trailed the Stanley Cup Finals series 3-2 against the New Jersey Devils.

Colorado lost Game 5 at home, 4-1. Afterward, Bourque and goaltender Patrick Roy sat together at a press conference. Both men wore a look of determination. The Avs had to win the next game on the road to extend the series. Bourque glanced at me as he exited the arena. He smiled and nodded after I said, "I'll see you Saturday" — which would happen only if the Avs won Game 6 in New Jersey. Bourque delivered a powerful pre-game speech,

IF YOU DON'T BELIEVE ME...

and Colorado won the game 4-0. The Avs returned home and won Game 7 by a score of 3-1—the same final score I predicted for an Avs win in my column on game day.

Long after the pandemonium had died down inside Pepsi Center, Bourque walked toward his family members standing outside of the Avs' locker room. Holding a can of beer, Bourque looked toward me, sighed and said, "I'm the man!" We laughed and looked for a place to take a picture together.

Bourque suggested we enter the team's private dressing room, which always has been off-limits to the press. There we were, first-time Stanley Cup champion Raymond Bourque and I, smiling while his sister, Rita, snapped the photo of us standing in the shower of the Avs' private dressing room.

♦ ♦ ♦

The dressing room can be a place for celebration. It can be a place for letting out frustration, too. That was the case for Boston Celtics legend Larry Bird on February 17, 1988. That night, the Celtics lost 138-125 to the Denver Nuggets at McNichols Sports Arena. Bird left town struggling to breathe the Mile High air after suffering a broken nose during the game.

I worked a side gig as an intern for a local radio station, and was granted a credential to the game from the Nuggets for the purpose of taping post-game interviews. The sports director would use some sound bites during his updates the following morning.

In the second quarter, Bird drove to the basket where he encountered Nuggets center Blair Rasmussen. Rasmussen's arms were raised when he felt Bird's face hit his left elbow. Bird was called for an offensive foul on the play and had to leave the game to receive medical attention. He played little during the second half, finishing with only 13 points—17 less than his season's average.

Afterward, a throng of reporters gathered by Bird's locker. The only open space I could find to join in the media gathering was in front of the empty locker next to Bird's stall. So I sat down and held a tape recorder's microphone from close range while Bird answered questions about being whistled for five fouls—including one that busted his beak.

"I was surprised at a lot of the calls—I've never been screwed so many times in my life," Bird told reporters. While Bird spoke, drops of blood from his nose landed repeatedly on my right shirt sleeve. I didn't realize it until he apologized. Afterward, Bird offered to sign his page inside my Celtics media guide—and handed me a can of Coors Light.

I drove home, drinking warm beer while wearing a shirt still moist from Larry Bird's bloody nose. I guess that night gave me a strange taste of what the "Good Life" could be from working in media.

Know When to Say Win

*"Why do I want to win it?
For one, I'm a winner."*

~Willie McGinest

Karen is the second-oldest of my three sisters — and the first of them to rub me the wrong way *all* the time. I might have been delivered into this world just so she would have a male sibling to antagonize.

Karen knew how to get into my head and push the emotional buttons — especially when it came to competing. She was bigger, smarter and better at everything. Just ask her, and I'm sure she'll confirm. Karen beat me in foot-races. She beat in board games.

She won everything *all* the time. She even created an annoying ditty to tease me about the shape of my skull. It remains stuck in my head today — 'Hump-hump hump head, hump-hump hump head ... '

The one game Karen loved to beat me at was checkers. She would win — and then remind me of her streak of consecutive victories.

"96, 97, 98 ... "

The memory of me finally ending Karen's long streak of wins in checkers still is fresh after 40 years. I had more kings on the board than Persia during Biblical times. Karen still had one move to make, but it wasn't the one I expected. She turned over the checkerboard. The sound of my kings crashing to the floor in the TV room was devastating. To widen the wound, Karen claimed a no-contest because the game didn't end properly.

So I punched her in the stomach.

I learned three things that evening. One, Karen was a sore loser. Two, my father didn't care for boys hitting girls. After he gave me a whipping, I was a sore winner. Three? Winning isn't everything, but it sure beats the heck out of losing. Big Sister No. 2 had a thing for winning all the time. I did too. Still do. It's the reason why my son Andrew never has beaten me playing one-on-one basketball. I couldn't let him win — and never will because I won't play him any more.

◆ ◆ ◆

WINNER AT GREAT AMERICAN COMEDY FESTIVAL

I took up comedy in 2001, at age 41. My mentor, Darryl Collier, told me that at some point I'd need to win a contest to legitimize my resume. It took a few years, but in 2009 I won at the Great American Comedy Festival in Norfolk (pronounced Nor-*fork*), Nebraska—childhood home of Johnny Carson.

It was the festival's "amateur" division competition. I really didn't see myself as an "amateur" since I had eight years of experience—at least five years more than most of the comedians in the field. The reality was, if I had lost to those comics with less experience, it would have been a bitter and humbling outcome to accept.

I didn't lose.

Fate allowed me an opportunity to compete in the festival's "pro" division, where the comics were hand-picked for the competition. One of 20 chosen comics took ill, and festival officials offered me the opportunity to step in. I accepted, and my world turned upside down.

Actually, my world already was upside down. Four months earlier, my bosses came to Denver to immediately shut down the *Rocky Mountain News*. I was in Norfolk with no full-time job, a $500 check and a gold-painted statue from winning GAFC's amateur comedy contest—with an opportunity to win an additional $5,000 by finishing in first place against the "pros."

For years, "pros" to me meant athletes. I was going up against pro comics whose resumes include appearances on Showtime, HBO, Letterman, Leno and Last Comic Standing. I was one of eight comics who advanced to the finals, which were judged by comedy legends Bill Dana and David Brenner. The winner, Kermet Apio, was a very deserving champion. I surprised a lot of people by finishing second, but adulation I felt from the audience made me feel like a winner, too—not to mention a second-place check worth $3,000.

◆   ◆   ◆

Often times during my career as a sports writer I was reminded of how repugnant losing could be for athletes. The Green Bay Packers played the New England Patriots in Super Bowl XXXI in New Orleans. A reporter asked Patriots linebacker Willie McGinest why he wanted to win the game.

"And once you've been there, (winning is) like a drug, man— you've got to have it. It's addicting. I figured if I did my job, we were going to (win.) Winning takes a backseat to nothing else."
~Rich "Goose" Gossage

McGinest replied, "For one, I'm a winner. I don't like losing. If anyone likes losing I don't think they should be competing at all in any type of sport or whatever they do ... And those big (rings) that go on your finger with all the diamonds in it is another reason."

The Patriots lost the game, but McGinest would go on to win three Super Bowls playing for the Patriots before his 15-year career ended with the Cleveland Browns in 2008.

Hall of Fame pitcher Rich "Goose" Gossage saved 310 Major League Baseball games—which meant 310 times some other pitcher received credit for winning the game.

IF YOU DON'T BELIEVE ME...

"What it boils down to isn't wins, losses or saves—I never was a stat man," Gossage once told me. "It was how did we do as a team. If we didn't go to the playoffs or go to the World Series I was disappointed.

"And once you've been there, (winning is) like a drug, man—you've got to have it. It's addicting. I figured if I did my job, we were going to (win). Winning takes a backseat to nothing else.

"It's the No. 1 thing."

There is a gap which separates the great performers from the rest of the field. It's created by an unbreakable will that usually bears itself in the most critical moments of competition. In some cases, it's a will that is born from a fear of losing.

The great performers seem able to utilize their fears to supplement their desires to succeed.

"You overcome fear with arrogance and with confidence that borders on arrogance."

~ Tim McKyer,
Three-time Super Bowl champion

Former defensive back Tim McKyer, a three-time Super Bowl champion during his 12-year NFL career, told me it's called the "Fear Zone" for football players. "You overcome the fear with arrogance and with confidence that borders on arrogance," McKyer said. "You know what I'm saying? This is *our* game—let's go take it. You get 46 guys thinking like that, your chances of winning are out the roof."

Players receive the money and glory. If the team doesn't produce more wins, usually it's the head coach and manager who bear the brunt of an owner's wrath. In a conversation I had once with the late Tom Landry, he stated bluntly, "You get respect when you win." Landry's teams won 250 regular-season games — the third-highest total for a coach in NFL history behind Don Shula (328) and the late George Halas (318).

Only six head coaches in NFL history have led their teams to back-to-back Super Bowl victories — Vince Lombardi (Green Bay), Don Shula (Miami), Chuck Noll (twice with Pittsburgh), Jimmy Johnson (Dallas), Mike Shanahan (Denver) and Bill Belichick (New England). I've been fortunate to have held extended conversations with Shula and Noll — a pair of Hall of Famers who have six Super Bowl championship wins between them.

Noll is the only head coach in NFL history to win four Super Bowls.

"It's hard to get there for one, period," Noll once told me. "It's not an easy trick."

No coach in any sport intrigued me more than Shanahan during my career as a reporter. Having spent so much time around him during his tenure in Denver, I was able to watch him closely at work. The man maintains an insatiable obsession for winning.

When a coach gets a reputation, as Shanahan has earned, for being a genius, guru — or "Mastermind" as my former *News* colleague Mike Littwin dubbed him — he must be obsessed with winning. It's hard for me to criticize Shanahan harshly. He truly is one of the nicest men I've ever met. Charming fellow. Knows exactly how to work a crowd. I've seen it first-hand time and time again.

At a fundraiser for underprivileged youth, I, as emcee, tried to persuade Shanahan to show his dance moves in front of an audience to raise additional monies during the live auction. He declined my idea, then took off his boots, removed his wallet and watch, and offered to jump fully-clothed off a diving springboard into an adjacent swimming pool.

If You Don't Believe Me...

Twenty people—including myself—paid $500 apiece to see it happen. Shanahan got on the springboard, jumped and executed a one-and-a-half (actually more like one-and-an-eighth) for $10,000.

That was "Nice Mike." But there was "Competitive Mike" too. I had an opportunity to play a round of golf with "Competitive Mike" once at Castle Pines Golf Club in suburban Denver. Jack Nicklaus designed the course. I butchered it while playing with Shanahan.

Honestly, it was a frustrating afternoon on a number of levels. "Competitive Mike" knew he was a far better golfer than I. Yet he still couldn't resist poking fun at my game. It took a par putt to win the 16th hole for me to prove to "Competitive Mike" that I could handle his irritating-but-good-natured jabs.

"Competitive Mike" even teased me about my choice of vodka at the end of the round. He ordered Grey Goose on the rocks. I asked for Skyy—which apparently is 'ghetto' on the country club circuit. "See, we only deal with the good stuff here," he teased. "Why don't you just ask for some Mad Dog 20/20?"

By the time I left the golf course I was certain that my prior beliefs about "Competitive Mike" were true—he thoroughly enjoyed playing mind games. If you couldn't handle them, you probably wouldn't make his team.

I always sensed there was a "Darth Mike" when it came to running a football team. He was the Broncos' head coach and executive vice-president of football operations. He had power and wasn't afraid to wield it. The players knew it, and I believe more than a few of them were uncomfortable from it. "Darth Mike" was the 16 hours-a-day coachaholic who expected every player to play hard on every play—and play hurt, if not injured. "Darth Mike" put running back Terrell Davis in to play during Super Bowl XXXII while Davis was blinded from a migraine headache.

"Darth Mike" wasn't afraid to attack a player's wallet—or ego—if he didn't produce at the coach's high standards. When he thought quarterback Bubby Brister wasn't getting the job done during preseason games in 1999, "Darth Mike" benched the veteran in favor of untested second-year quarterback Brian Griese. It was a move that angered the Broncos' veterans, but "Darth Mike" stuck with his decision.

> *"He loved to attack a defense and embarrass them. During the week he would talk like, 'Oh, we're going to kill these guys. You don't understand—we're going to thrash them.' And then we'd go out on a Sunday, and we would do what he told us was going to happen. It was amazing."*
> — Steve Young,
> Hall of Fame quarterback

Shanahan was one of a handful of NFL coaches who had the final say in personnel decisions. "The toughest decision nowadays is dealing with the salary cap," Shanahan told me during an interview for *Colorado AvidGolfer* magazine. "There are guys that you like and you respect because they're great people. But you know from a business standpoint some of them might be at the tail-end of their careers, or their game is going down.

"You have to cut his salary—or you have to cut the player because he's not playing at the level now that you'd like him to play at ... You have that loyalty toward that player, but when you do, you have to do what's best for the team. So there's a fine line there, where you've got to make decisions based solely on financial and fiscal responsibility.

"That's tough, as a head coach, when you're involved in those decisions."

Hall of Fame quarterback Steve Young won a Super Bowl ring with the San Francisco 49ers in the 1994 season. Shanahan was the team's offensive coordinator, and Young was enamored with his relentless desire to dominate an opponent.

"He was intense in the preparation and he was aggressive," Young once told me. "He loved to attack a defense and embarrass them. During the week he would talk like, 'Oh, we're going to kill these guys. You don't understand—we're going to thrash them.' And then we'd go out on a Sunday, and we would do what he told us was going to happen. It was amazing.

"He has tremendous confidence, and he really believes in his game plans. Like, when he comes out with a game plan on Wednesday, it was as if it came from heaven. It was like this thing is pure, you know what I mean? This thing is going to kill them. And he would stand up and he would say, 'Here's the defensive coordinator. This is his name, and this is what he's going to do and this is how we're going to kill him.' And then it would happen.

"And so I thought it was pretty unique. He was very confident. I liked that."

♦ ♦ ♦

The Broncos finished 8-8 in 1995—Shanahan's first season as the team's head coach. The following year Denver finished the regular season with an AFC-best 13 wins, but suffered an embarrassing playoff loss at home to the Jacksonville Jaguars. It was a loss that, to me anyways, seemed to bring out a ruthlessness from "Darth Mike" the offensive play-caller in the following season. The Broncos' offense scored with machine-like precision throughout the '97 season en route to a Super Bowl XXXII trip to San Diego, where they defeated the Green Bay Packers 31-24.

In 1998, Denver won its first 14 games, with an offense that produced 58 touchdowns on the season. The Broncos won Super Bowl XXXIII in Miami, 34-19, giving Shanahan consecutive Super Bowl championship victories.

Lombardi, Shula, Noll are Pro Football Hall of Famers. Johnson isn't a likely Hall inductee with only 80 regular-season wins in his NFL coaching career. Belichick, with three Super Bowl wins in five Super Bowl appearances as a head coach, is a shoo-in for enshrinement.

Shanahan, who is in his fourth season with the Washington Redskins, ranks 12th on the list for most regular-season NFL coaching wins with 167. One would expect him to get the Hall of Fame nod because of his career regular-season win total plus multiple Super Bowl victories—three, if you count the Super Bowl XXIX win as a 49ers' assistant.

Dan Reeves, who hired Shanahan as an assistant coach with the Broncos in 1984, is eighth on the all-time list with 190 regular-season coaching wins. Reeves' 201 wins (including playoffs) is ninth-best all-time. But he went 0-4 as a head coach in Super Bowls—including the loss to Shanahan's Broncos in Super Bowl XXXIII—which is impeding his induction into the Hall of Fame.

♦ ♦ ♦

If You Don't Believe Me...

Like Reeves, Shanahan's coaching successes in Denver always have been attached to the right arm of quarterback John Elway. It has been said many times that Shanahan wouldn't have won Super Bowl rings in Denver without Elway at quarterback. Then again, Elway didn't win his championship rings without Shanahan.

The Elway-Shanahan 'Who wouldn't win a Super Bowl without who' argument always has come with a 'Which came first—the chicken or the egg?' feel to it. But it's duly noted that neither would have those Super Bowl championships if not for the talents of running back Terrell Davis.

To take it a step further, there was talk long after Elway's retirement that his once-iron strong relationship with Shanahan had gone sour. Whenever the subject of Elway re-joining the Broncos in a front office capacity was broached, the counter was that Shanahan, who also held the title of executive vice-president of football operations, wouldn't allow his former quarterback the opportunity to veto any say from "Darth Mike" the head coach.

It seemed like a ridiculous notion—but one which might have carried a small trace of merit. Shanahan didn't come off as the kind of guy who wanted to be told what to do. Even though Pat Bowlen (and his family) owns the Broncos, to some it seemed as if "Darth Mike" controlled the direction of the franchise.

Bowlen shocked the NFL by firing Shanahan at the end of the 2008 season. In 2011 he hired Elway to fill Shanahan's former role as the Broncos' executive VP of football operations. Fourteen years coaching one team was a pretty impressive feat, but I thought it was time for Shanahan to move on. Not that there's a direct correlation, but it seemed like "Nice Mike" was building a lavish suburban home and "Competitive Mike" was opening a swank new steakhouse but "Darth Mike" was producing average results on the football field—24-24 in his final three seasons.

Elway and Shanahan were a lethal player-coach tandem. It's too bad they never connected in a front office relationship, or Broncos' fans might already have a few more Super Bowl victories to brag about. Both know pro football—and each other—too well not to succeed together.

"We have a lot of the same personality flaws," Shanahan once told me.

Shanahan's firing in Denver was a reminder that the NFL, like all of professional sports, is a "What-have-you-won-for-me-lately?" business. If your team is not winning, turn the checkerboard over and wipe the slate clean.

Make No Mistake

"Once you get to it and you can smell being world champs, the more you want it."

~John Elway

The Cleveland Browns beat the Los Angeles Rams to win the National Football League championship in 1950. It was the same year my parents were married. The NFL's yearly standings also show the Browns played for championships when my mother was pregnant with girls.

My eldest sister Saundra was born in 1952. That year, the Browns lost the NFL title game 17-7 to the Detroit Lions. Sister No. 2, Karen, was born in 1955. That year, the Browns beat the Rams 38-14 for the league championship. Cheryl, the youngest of the trio, was born in 1964. That year, the Browns beat the Baltimore Colts 27-0. It was the last time a major pro sports team in Cleveland won a league championship.

Guess I missed out on our family's NFL championship game gene. The year I was born (1960) the Browns finished in second place with an 8-3-1 record.

The Philadelphia Eagles won the NFL title in 1960. That same year, the United States' men's basketball team won Olympic gold in Rome, Italy — as did a talented U.S. light-heavyweight boxer named Cassius Clay. Bill Mazeroski's leadoff solo home run in the bottom of the ninth inning of Game 7 gave the Pittsburgh Pirates a 1960 World Series championship series victory over the New York Yankees. The Boston Celtics won the NBA title and the Montreal Canadiens won the NHL's Stanley Cup in 1960.

John F. Kennedy was elected President of the United States in 1960. Ben-Hur won Best Motion Picture at the 1960 Academy Awards. Arnold Palmer came back from a 7-stroke deficit in the final round to win golf's U.S. Open at Denver's Cherry Hills Country Club.

The Denver Broncos played their first season in the American Football League in 1960 — the same year their future Hall of Fame quarterback was born.

John Albert Elway tortured the souls of Browns fans throughout his NFL career. I am one of those poor souls. To clarify, I was a rabid fan of the Browns who played in Cleveland *before* being moved to Baltimore in 1996 by owner Art Modell. I never have rooted for the Baltimore Ravens — and probably never will embrace the "new" Browns.

If You Don't Believe Me...

◆ ◆ ◆

For me, letting go of the Browns had every bit as much to do with the citizens of Cleveland as it did the decision by Modell to move the team to Baltimore. Both the Browns and Cleveland Indians shared use of decrepit Municipal Stadium. As a kid, I attended Indians games at the stadium. I sold popcorn, soda, hot dogs and beer at Indians and Browns games. The place was a dump. It was time for change.

In the spring of 1984, a $150 million bond issue for a new domed stadium appeared on the county ballot. On election morning, I stood outside a local cleaners passing out stickers that had a domed stadium on it, asking people to vote "Yes."

The issue was voted down by more than 130,000 votes — a 2-to-1 margin. To me, it was the ultimate Mistake by the Lake. I understood times were tough economically, but I truly was disappointed that most Clevelanders didn't see the benefit of financially supporting a new sports facility.

In 1996, after Modell relocated the Browns to Baltimore, Cleveland voters approved a sin tax for funding of a new stadium — a facility that was necessary for the NFL to return to Cleveland. In 1999, the Browns were back in the league. They would play their home games at the new Cleveland Browns Stadium.

I have to believe Modell, who died in 2012, never would have moved the team if a new domed stadium had been approved in 1984. Playing in a domed stadium would have allowed Modell — who was one of the NFL's most powerful owners — to influence his league brethren to bring a Super Bowl to Cleveland. If Detroit received rights to host the NFL's championship game, so could Cleveland with the addition of a domed stadium.

In 1982, Detroit hosted Super Bowl XVI at the Pontiac Silverdome (as well as Super Bowl XL at domed Ford Field in 2006.)

The disappointment felt from the election result, coupled with the fact that I was a 24-year-old man still living with my parents, were the primary reasons for my decision to move out of Cleveland. In September of '84, I packed my belongings and took a Greyhound bus to Denver. The "Go West, young man" theory appealed to me. I also had two friends living in the area who felt it would be a good place to settle.

I was ready to get to know Denver. Denver, meanwhile, still was getting to know Elway.

There is a "Me-Cleveland-Elway" thing that requires explanation. It actually began in 1983, during Elway's rookie season.

On November 27, 1983, the Broncos lost 31-7 at San Diego. Elway's post-game interview was seen nationally. The dude mumbled badly while tucked in his locker, surrounded by reporters with recorders, microphones and note pads. It's the kind of body language rookie quarterbacks show after throwing three interceptions and being sacked four times. I had no mercy for the guy. They lost badly to the Chargers, and the following Sunday Elway would face my Browns in Denver.

Wouldn't you know it? Elway threw for 284 yards and two touchdowns. The Broncos hammered Cleveland 27-6. Both teams finished the season at 9-7, but the win over the Browns gave the Broncos a wild-card playoff berth.

Elway 1, Cleveland 0

"He went through some very tough times," former Broncos linebacker Tom Jackson told me. "It seems to me that much of that (1983) season, for him, was a character-building season for a rookie who was very talented and having to feel his way through the NFL."

I've become friendly with Jackson over the years, a connection made through our ties with media. We have one other tie — we're both native Clevelanders.

If You Don't Believe Me...

♦ ♦ ♦

My arrival in Denver in '84 was not without drama. Greyhound lost my suitcase, so I went to a downtown temp agency wearing a sweatsuit and tennis shoes. I passed a clerical skills test and was put to work immediately as a night processor at a downtown bank. The first night on the gig, I learned about Bronco-mania. My co-workers were dressed in orange and blue and rooting hard for the Broncos, who were playing a nationally-televised game ... in Cleveland.

The Browns led 14-0 before Elway threw two second-quarter touchdown passes to tie the game. Randy Robbins' fourth-quarter interception return for a touchdown sealed Denver's 24-14 win.

Elway 2, Cleveland 0

♦ ♦ ♦

The Broncos had a great regular season in '84, finishing 13-3 before losing to the Pittsburgh Steelers in a divisional playoff game. The following year, Cleveland won the AFC Central Division title with an 8-8 record. The Broncos, at 11-5, finished second in the AFC West but missed the playoffs because of a league tie-breaker.

In the 1986 season, the Browns and Broncos met in the AFC Championship Game played at Cleveland.

The Browns led 20-13 after quarterback Bernie Kosar connected with receiver Brian Brennan on a 48-yard touchdown pass play. I was certain they were going to Super Bowl XXI. The Broncos got the football back at their 2-yard line with five minutes and thirty-two seconds left in regulation.

"We really had nothing to lose at that point because nobody really gave us chance," Elway would tell me nearly 10 years later. I was one of the many non-believers.

Fourteen plays and six first downs later, the Broncos were lined up on Cleveland's 5-yard line, needing one yard to pick up a first down with 39 seconds. Elway shunned the one yard and threw a fastball into the end zone that sent receiver Mark Jackson diving to the stadium turf to make a touchdown catch.

"I'd never thrown a ball that hard in my life," Elway recalled.

I never slammed my fist onto a floor so hard as I did when Jackson made the catch. The game was tied at 20, and the deafening silence at Cleveland's Municipal Stadium could be heard on television sets across the country — except in the Rocky Mountain region, where sounds of pandemonium raged.

The Broncos went on to win 23-20 in overtime when Ohio native Rich Karlis kicked a 33-yard field goal.

Elway 3, Cleveland 0

◆ ◆ ◆

"I kept looking at the look on his face when he kept coming to the sideline. It was somewhere between real, real focused and real, real crazed. People talk about being in the zone. (Elway) was right there."

~Tom Jackson

If You Don't Believe Me...

"'The Drive' was 'The Drive,'" Tom Jackson told me. "Cleveland just happened to be the team. I don't know whether anybody could have stopped John that day ... It's a thing of beauty. I kept looking at the look on his face when he kept coming to the sideline. It was somewhere between real, real focused and real, real crazed. People talk about being in the zone. (Elway) was right there."

The 1987 NFL regular season was cut short a game due to a players' strike. The game canceled on the Browns' schedule was a rematch against the Broncos in Cleveland. The two teams would meet again in the playoffs—only this time in Denver. It was a game remembered most for "The Fumble." Cleveland running back Earnest Byner fumbled at the Broncos' 2-yard line late in the fourth quarter, and Denver won the '87 AFC Championship Game 38-33.

Elway 4, Cleveland 0

"It's real funny. Cleveland wasn't a big deal for us until we noticed we were beating them all the time," Tom Jackson told me. "And I don't know if it ever became a big deal for us. It was a big deal for them because they were on the losing end of those games."

Two years later, the Browns finally beat Denver and Elway, 16-13 in a wacky regular season game played in Cleveland. At one point during the fourth quarter Browns fans pelted Broncos players with an assortment of objects. Referee Tom Dooley allowed the teams to switch ends of the field.

When it counted most in the 1989 season, the Broncos punished Cleveland 37-21 in the AFC Championship Game.

Elway 5, Cleveland 1

◆ ◆ ◆

The Browns made it 5-2 against Elway in 1990 after beating Denver at Mile High Stadium, 30-29 on a last-second field goal. The count grew to 6-2 in 1991, when Elway threw two touchdowns in a 17-7 win at Cleveland, and 7-2 after a 12-0 Broncos win at Cleveland in 1992.

The Broncos were mired in a four-game losing streak late in the '92 season. Elway missed all four losses with a shoulder injury. Denver had a 7-7 record and still was in the hunt for a playoff berth.

Elway was at the team's training facility ready to proclaim himself fit to return to the lineup. I was dispatched by *The Denver Post* to the Broncos' practice facility to get his comments.

We were introduced on Sunday, December 13, not knowing that the next year—and for years to follow—we would see a lot more of one another. As time passed between "The Drive" in the '86 AFC title game and Elway win No. 7 over the Browns in '92, I had worked my way into the ranks of full-time employment at the Post. In 1993, the paper assigned me to the Broncos' beat.

In a delightfully fiendish—and mildly cruel—twist of fate, I had a job requiring that I see John Elway on a regular basis. The reporter in me couldn't wait to let Elway know just how much hate the Browns fan within me was harboring. That moment occurred on November 5, 1993—two days before the Broncos played the Browns in Cleveland.

Broncos coach Wade Phillips was holding a post-practice press conference when I spotted Elway heading toward the locker room. I left Phillips and tailed Elway. He was hunched over at his locker, loosening cleat laces when he noticed me hovering over him. Elway asked what I wanted, and I let him know.

"My mother hates you, my sisters hate you, my cousins hate you, my friends hate you ... "

If You Don't Believe Me...

A puzzled look settled on his face as I finished the rant. *"Yeah, I'm from Cleveland."* Elway went back to tending to his cleats, looked up again and said, "You're from Cleveland? I'm sorry." He cackled as I left the locker room burning mad.

The Broncos won 29-14, with Elway throwing three touchdown passes. Afterward I approached him in the visitors' locker room and sarcastically asked why he continued the pattern of walking out of Municipal Stadium with wins. Elway laughed and said, "I guess it was because I knew you were a native ... I did it for your mom."

Elway 8, Cleveland 2

♦ ♦ ♦

That brief locker room exchange was the turning point for me. The Browns fan in me still hated Elway. But the reporter in me saw a guy who wanted to win so badly that he didn't care whose feelings got hurt—even if those hurt feelings belonged to *your* mother.

In Elway's first seven seasons, the Broncos beat the Browns three times in conference championship games—only to lose in Super Bowls by scores of 39-20, 42-10 and 55-10. While Cleveland fans wallowed in pitiful memories of "The Drive" and "The Fumble", Broncos fans were shell-shocked from "The Beatings"—136-40 in three Super Bowls.

Elway had earned a reputation around the league as a one-man band.

"I think that the biggest mistakes that we made during the 1980s were that we had probably one of the greatest offensive weapons in the game in John Elway and we didn't build around him," Broncos owner Pat Bowlen told me in 1993. "We expected John to do things within the system, rather than taking the system and tailoring it to John.

"He's the one guy we can't win without."

SAM ADAMS

Hall of Famer Bart Starr once said of Elway, "Here's a man who carried his team single-handedly for years. I don't know if there are enough fitting descriptions out there for what this guy has done. When you talk about courage, there is not a person who has ever played who had any more than he has."

As the 1993 season continued, I became more enamored with watching Elway compete on the football field. His knack for making big plays at the end of games was reaching legendary status, but Elway made plays early in games that were equally jaw-dropping and worthy of praise.

The only time I've been admonished for cheering in a press box happened at the Kingdome in Seattle, on November 28, 1993. The Broncos had the ball at midfield to start the second quarter, needing to pick up at least 18 yards on a third down play. The Kingdome, probably the noisiest venue in pro football, had more than 57,000 people screaming at the top of their lungs. Elway, playing on a gimpy right foot, stood in the shotgun formation while facing Seattle's defense.

Seahawks linebacker David Brandon rushed up the middle, untouched with a clear path to hit Elway. He whiffed on the chance. Elway ducked and shedded Brandon, then straightened himself upright at the Broncos' 43-yard line and fired a pass deep downfield. Tight end Shannon Sharpe caught the ball in stride at Seattle's 6-yard line and continued running across the goal line.

Two future Hall of Famers—Elway and Sharpe—had collaborated on a scoring play so remarkable that I jumped out of my seat and yelled—a no-no in NFL press boxes. I couldn't help it. It was—and remains to this day—the best football play I've ever witnessed. Denver won the game 17-9. The level of admiration and appreciation I held for Elway's competitive drive was rising to new heights.

Denver finished the regular season 9-7 in '93, and lost a wild-card playoff game to the L.A. Raiders.

If You Don't Believe Me...

♦ ♦ ♦

Expectations were high in 1994, both for the Broncos and for me covering the team. I took over the lead on the *Post's* two-man beat.

I had become comfortable with being around the players during the season, as well as monitoring all the issues away from the football field that required constant attention in the off-season—free-agent signings, contract renegotiations, trade rumors, coaching staff changes, draft prospects and the new salary cap instituted by the league in '94. I couldn't wait for the new season to begin.

I went to a bar one night during Broncos' training camp in Greeley. Elway was there with some teammates, and I settled at their table to drink beers. I left the group quick after noticing the bar had a Pop-a-Shot basketball machine. I *loved* playing Pop-a-Shot basketball. For me, it was a 50-cent high.

For 50 cents, a Pop-a-Shot machine would give you 45 seconds to score as many baskets as possible. Each basket made during the first 30 seconds counts for two points, and three points for each made shot during the last 15 seconds of the game. I shot one game alone before Elway, to my surprise, came to the machine and challenged me.

I didn't know which "me" wanted to whip Elway more—the "reporter me" or the "Browns fan me."

I was certain of one thing—neither one of "me" was going to lose. I didn't know—or care— how good he might be at the game.

We flipped a coin to see who would go first. I lost. The quarters were in, the buzzer sounded and I started shooting balls into the basket, one after another. With five seconds left I glanced at Elway while shooting baskets. I couldn't miss—even when I didn't look at the basket. If only I had a camera to capture the look of dejection on his face. Elway *knew* he couldn't beat my score. His turn, really, was a waste of 45 seconds.

Adams 82, Elway 36

To my count, the margin of victory was larger (by one point) than the Broncos' worst Super Bowl loss. I had competed against John Elway and won. There was no rematch that night — and there never will be one. It would serve as an ominous sign of things to come for Elway in '94, as the Broncos started the regular season at 0-4.

The Broncos hosted the Browns at Mile High Stadium on October 30, 1994. Elway completed 31 of 40 passes for 349 yards and two touchdowns, and Denver won the game 26-14.

Elway 9, Cleveland 2

♦ ♦ ♦

The win over Cleveland was a much-needed elixir for a Broncos team that finished the '94 season at 7-9. Bowlen made a coaching change for the second time in three years, replacing Phillips with Mike Shanahan in 1995.

I experienced change too, leaving the Post to work for *The Charlotte Observer* in 1995. The Broncos finished 8-8 in the '95 season. In '96 I returned to Denver to cover the team again — this time working for the *Rocky Mountain News*.

I looked forward to being around the Broncos for the '96 season. The team's passion to win a championship was easy to detect — especially during a nine-game winning streak that included a 45-34 win over the Baltimore Ravens — who used to be the Cleveland Browns.

Elway 10, Modell 2

♦ ♦ ♦

If You Don't Believe Me...

I learned a lot about Elway after the Broncos' shocking loss at home to the Jacksonville Jaguars in the 1996 playoffs. He faced the media afterward, answering every question thrown his way while trying to mask the obvious hurt he felt from within. The loss to Jacksonville dug deep into Elway's football gut and, at age 37, he knew his opportunities to win a Super Bowl were dwindling to a precious few. Losing in such a devastating manner seemed to galvanize Elway's commitment to put the Broncos in position to win a championship.

"It's easy when you lose one," Elway once told me. "I think the closer you get to it, and once you get to it and you can smell being world champs, the more you want it. For guys that have been to a Super Bowl and lost, there's as much drive, if not more in them than there is for a guy who never has been to one—because he doesn't know what it's like."

The Broncos went to back-to-back Super Bowls in 1997 and 1998, beating the Green Bay Packers in Super Bowl XXXII and the Dan Reeves-coached Atlanta Falcons 34-19 in Super Bowl XXXIII. Elway announced his retirement on May 1, 1999. On August 8, 2004 he was enshrined at the Pro Football Hall of Fame in Canton, Ohio—60 miles south of Cleveland. He sent me an invitation to attend the induction ceremony. Respectfully and reluctantly, I turned down the invitation—fearing the inner Browns fan in me might cause a scene. Well, that and my family and friends might show up to pelt him with dog bones for old time's sake.

I have to say it was a privilege to watch and report on the career of John Elway. To me, he is one of the all-time greatest competitors in the history of professional sports. My time spent rooting for the Cleveland Browns would have been just fine without Elway. With him, my career as a sports writer was made complete.

AFTERWORD

"This life is really hard.
Sometimes it's easier to give up
when you think there's no hope.
That's when you try your
hardest. That's when you win,
because you don't give up."
— the late Jennifer Enoch-Hale

The first time I stepped on a stage to perform comedy was Tuesday, May 15, 2001. It was "New Talent Night" at Denver's famed Comedy Works. First-timers get two minutes on stage. I looked at the audience and delivered this jewel: "I knew this was going to happen ... I forgot everything I wanted to say." The audience laughed. The next line was, "How about those (Colorado) Avalanche? ... Leave it to the black guy to bring up hockey." More laughter. The next 90 seconds were dull, but the audience was sensitive to new beginnings and offered a kind round of applause at the end of my set.

A career in comedy was born, and it's been growing ever since. Turning to stand-up comedy has been extremely challenging. First off, I don't get sarcasm. I'm extremely gullible—which means often times, others make me the butt of jokes that I don't even understand. But I've managed to survive and thrive on stage.

I've stood in front of 30 people to perform my routine at a bar in North Dakota, and told jokes in front of 9,000 people at an amphitheater in Colorado. I've performed in front of Joe Schmo in Ohio, Jose Schmo in New Mexico and an audience full of sports greats like Magic Johnson, Kareem Abdul-Jabbar, James Worthy and Dave Winfield in California. I've done well enough with comedy to almost convince myself that I don't miss covering sports.

I don't miss writing on deadline. I don't miss creating stories, writing stories or chasing stories. I don't miss the free press passes, free parking or free press box food. I'm cool with sitting on the couch and watching the games from the comfort of my home. But on a few occasions I have thought about how cool it would be to get back on the inside again, talking to players after a game or before practice to find out what's really going on.

Those thoughts usually dissipate after the fourth vodka.

The further I am removed from sports reporting, the funnier I find the media's overkill in reporting sports to be. The amount of attention paid to things that have nothing to do with the actual art of team and individual competition borders on ridiculous—things like contract negotiations, hirings and firings, arrests, romantic relationships and social media habits.

Does anybody really know who won the game? Does anybody really care?

◆ ◆ ◆

During the research process for writing this book, I found a microcassette tape with the voice of Donnie Davis. Davis was a 22-year-old, fifth-year senior quarterback for Georgia Tech in 1995. During a preseason interview session with media covering the Atlantic Coast Conference, Davis was asked if he wanted to publicly express his frustrations from the previous season. He wouldn't take the bait.

"There are a lot worst things that can happen in life. Things can always be worse," Davis said. "Sometimes we just lose sight of what we have. It's very easy to do. We're on the field sometimes and you have coaches hollering at you—you might throw a bad pass here or drop a ball there ... The whole time, someone's walking (in the streets) just trying to find something to eat. Sometimes, we look at things in a perspective where, at that moment, we're thinking that's all that is important to us—that pass or that catch—when in (reality), there are things that are a lot bigger."

I believe Davis was right. So was Jennifer Enoch-Hale.

◆ ◆ ◆

I wrote a column about Enoch-Hale in 2000, two months after returning from my Olympics assignment in Sydney, Australia. She told me the story of her ongoing fight against cancer, how she looked forward to celebrating her 50th birthday and how she looked forward to spending Christmas with her family—including her sons David and Ryan Hale, both of whom played hockey for the University of North Dakota.

I spent nearly two hours with Enoch-Hale at a restaurant in Colorado Springs. Before leaving, she gave me a hug—and two unexpected gifts. One gift was a candle. The other gift came in the form of these inspirational words: *"This life is really hard. Sometimes it's easier to give up when you think there's no hope. That's when you try your hardest. That's when you win, because you don't give up."*

Enoch-Hale died September 6, 2001—seven months after celebrating her 50th birthday. I still have her candle. I still believe in her words.

After reminiscing and documenting so many experiences over the past two decades in this book, I've come to the conclusion that I was pretty dang lucky to have a job for 23 years covering sports, and to have crossed paths with people like Davis and Enoch-Hale.

I'm certain the spirit of my career in sports journalism will live on—no matter how hard I try to lay it to rest.

About The Author

Sam's career was nothing short of remarkable, not necessarily because of his accomplishments, but because of what he was uniquely privileged enough to witness along the way.

From insurance clerk to sports writer, sports writer to comedian ... and now, author. Sam Adams indeed is a Renaissance Man.

At age 24 in 1984, he moved from Cleveland, Ohio to Denver, Colorado, and worked jobs as an insurance clerk. Two years later he walked into the sports department of *The Denver Post* asking how he could become a sports writer. Biding his time as a part-time correspondent in the high school sports department, he gained experience and showed enough wares to earn a full-time job at the Post in 1992.

In 1995, he accepted a job at *The Charlotte Observer*, but returned to Denver 18 months later to work for the *Rocky Mountain News*—a job he held for 13 years. During his time at the News, he covered three Super Bowls, a Stanley Cup Finals, a World Series and two Olympiads, while earning awards—including Print Journalist of the Year from his peers in 2003.

Sam began performing comedy in 2001 at age 41. When the News closed in 2009, he decided to turn to comedy as a full-time career. That same year, he won at the Great American Comedy Festival. His clean, profanity-free performances have earned him numerous accolades in the corporate industry.

If you liked

IF YOU DON'T BELIEVE ME...

Please leave a review on Amazon.com

Also available in Kindle

To find out more about Sam Adams appearances please visit:

SamAdamsComedy.com

Made in the USA
Columbia, SC
20 April 2019